SCHOLASTIC CANADA

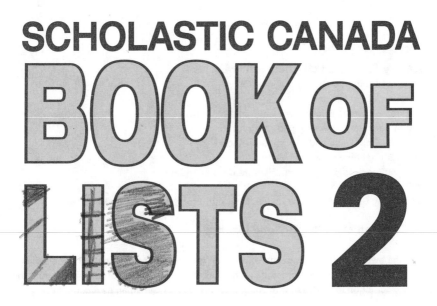

BOOK OF LISTS 2

By James Buckley, Jr. and Robert Stremme

with Carrie Gleason

Scholastic Canada Ltd.
Toronto New York London Auckland
Mexico City New Delhi Hong Kong Bue

Produced by Shoreline Publishing Group LLC

Santa Barbara, California

www.shorelinepublishing.com

Editorial Director: James Buckley, Jr.

Designed by Tom Carling, www.carlingdesign.com.

Illustrations by Chip Wass and Steckfigures, Inc.

Additional editorial help provided by

Beth Adelman (copy, additional text), Nanette Cardon (index),

and Jim Gigliotti (additional text).

Thanks to Danny Biederman (www.spyfiarchives.com) for the cool list on page 180.

Special Canadian contributor: Carrie Gleason

Thanks to the awesome Paula Manzanero (and the "geniuses in production") at Scholastic (USA) for putting up with wayward authors and laughing at all (well . . . most) of Jim's jokes. And thanks to Jennifer MacKinnon in Canada for making sure this was as Canadian as it could be!

Library and Archives Canada Cataloguing in Publication

Buckley, James, 1963-

Scholastic Canada book of lists 2 / James Buckley, Jr., Robert Stremme

ISBN 978-0-545-99038-7

1. Handbooks, vade-mecums, etc.--Juvenile literature. I. Stremme, Robert.

II. Title. II. Title: Book of lists two. III. Title: Scholastic Canada book of lists two.

AG106.B823 2009   j031.02   C2008-906877-7

6 5 4 3 2 1   Printed in Canada   09 10 11 12 13

Table of Contents

Introduction

We're back! Did you miss us? We had so much fun making the first *Scholastic Canada Book of Lists* — and so many of you had so much fun reading it — we decided to make another one! And so . . . welcome to the second entry on the list of *Scholastic Books of Lists* — Canada style!

In the first edition, we covered a lot of the basics: prime ministers, oceans, Grey Cup winners, bones, baby animals, popular movies, blah, blah, blah. Well . . . been there, done that! In this all-new edition, we've packed it with tons of really fun lists that will _____ you. (Please fill in the blank with one or more words from the following list of verbs.)

- thrill
- amaze
- stun
- entertain
- surprise
- startle
- tickle
- bother

As you can see, we just love lists. They're so handy and compact. They're so easy to organize and remember. They're so easily recognized by readers. They're so, well . . . cute! (Okay, maybe not the one on page 226 — your call.)

In *Scholastic Canada*

Book of Lists 2, you'll find all sorts of new, cool stuff. Knights (page 16) and days (page 253). Ups ("Shuttle Stuff," page 111) and downs (deepest caves, page 98). Garth Brooks (page 170) and famous cooks (page 242). We pass on gas (page 129) and hit a Homer (page 192). We've got La La and Ya Ya (page 207) and ha-ha (depending on your point of view, page 272). We've got niblicks and pharaohs and bivalves, oh my!

In this new edition, we've added a chapter all about food, so you can make your own list of what you'd like to use to "soup up" (see page 225) your school lunch menus. Look for tasty things like cow brain tacos, lobster ice cream, marigolds, and silkworm grubs! Mmm, mmm, good!

Oh, yes, indeed, there is a world of interesting info jam-packed into these colourful pages. Do you know what octophobia is? Check out page 255 (but don't look at the page to the left of this one if you've got it . . . aaaah!).

In various places throughout this book, you'll see boxes like this one. Here's where we'll try to ask — and answer — questions that might pop up in our minds (and, we hope, yours) about some of the info on the page. You might also see an exclamation point. It's all in an effort to add cool background stuff, contribute to your vast spread of knowledge, or just try to squeeze in a few more jokes.

Can you name the world's stinkiest plant (and no, it's not your sibling's socks)? Hold your nose and read page 133. Do you know why Lady Byng is a big name in hockey? She's never had a good slap shot, but you can see why she's important on page 292.

You can even find out where lanfairpwllgwyngyllgogerychw yrndrobwllllantysiliogogogoch is located.

So, does all this sound like more homework? Well, it's not. And to prove it, we've even put in some games, one at the end of each chapter, to let you have even more fun. Read over the lists, have fun with the games (the answers begin on page 318 if you want to cheat!), and make a list of all the things you like about the book. No matter how you use the book, remember: you're number one on our list.

Abbreviations Used in This Book

Most of the abbreviations used are for measurements. We're using both the metric and imperial systems. For more info, check out the conversion chart on page 116).

C	Celsius	l	litre	sq. mi.	square mile
F	Fahrenheit	lb.	pound		
ft.	foot	m	metre	tbs.	tablespoon
g	gram	oz.	ounce	tsp.	teaspoon
kg	kilogram	sq. km	square kilometre	yd.	yard
km	kilometre			in.	inch

CHAPTER ONE

History

Just because stuff happened before you were born doesn't mean it isn't important!
So, our present to you is a trip to the past.

History Periods

Scientists look at history in a different way than the rest of us. While we're busy trying to memorize dates (1497, 1867, etc.) or figure out who came first, the Romans or the Greeks, or to remember who won the Battle of the Bulge, paleontologists and other scientists are looking way, way, way, way back in the fossil record. They divide time not in mere years, but in "ages," "periods," "epochs," "eons," and other lengthy time periods. Here's a list, in order of most recent to oldest, of the "periods" into which history is divided by science. (Note: Some of the specific years noted might vary from source to source.)

NAME	MILLIONS OF YEARS AGO
Quaternary	today to 1.8
Tertiary	1.8–65
Cretaceous	65–146
Jurassic	146–208
Triassic	208–248
Permian	248–280
Carboniferous	280–360
Devonian	360–408
Silurian	408–438
Ordovician	438–505
Cambrian	505–540
Vendian/Ediacaran	540–600

Who Arrived First?

Was Columbus the first to set foot in America? Nope. Though his journey in 1492 (as well as John Cabot's in 1497, to what is now Canada) was important to the settling (or conquering, depending on your point of view) of the Americas, he was not first. People had been living here for thousands of years. Here's a list of some civilizations that were here before Columbus.

North America

Thousands of Aboriginal tribes, too numerous to list here, including those existing today and some that have disappeared, were living in what is now the United States and Canada.

Central America

The major civilizations included Aztec, Huastec, Maya, Mixtec, Olmec, Pipil, Tarascan, Teotihuacán, Toltec, Totonac, and Zapotec.

South America

Large civilizations or tribes included Chavín, Chibcha, Chimor, Chachapoya, Huari, Inca, Moche, Nazca, Tairona, and Tiawanaku.

Was Columbus Even First?

Many experts think that Vikings were actually the first Europeans to reach North America, perhaps about 1000 CE. Some stories say that Chinese explorers reached the west coast before Columbus arrived in the east. There are also some scholars who say sailors from the Islamic Empire or traders from West Africa arrived in North America as much as 500 years before ol' Christopher. Columbus got his own day in the United States, but the debate about him goes on.

GREAT
World Empires

For many centuries, the world was organized not by nations, but by empires. One group of people — usually led by one strong leader — conquered large swaths of territory, creating empires that stretched for thousands of kilometres. Of course, you couldn't vote to become part of an empire; it was pretty much decided for you. Empires rose and fell over the centuries, expanding into new areas and carrying their cultures with them. Here's a list of some of the most important or prominent . . . and here's hoping we don't see any new ones any time soon. (Note: The dates are approximate; they didn't all have starting and ending times like a movie or a modern country; for the most part, they grew slowly and faded over time.)

EMPIRE (LOCATIONS)	APPROX. DATES
Egyptian (Egypt/N. Africa)	3000 BCE–30 BCE
Greek (Europe/Middle East/N. Africa)	1500 BCE–150 BCE
Roman (Europe/Asia/N. Africa)	600 BCE–410
Macedonian* (Middle East/Asia)	330 BCE–310 BCE
Han (China)	200 BCE–220
Byzantine (Middle East/Asia)	400–1450

Arab/Islamic (Europe/Africa)   630–1250

Ghana (West Africa)   800–1200

Mongol# (India/Asia)   1100–1360

Inca (Central South America)   1200–1550

Mali (West Africa)   1250–1400

Ottoman (Middle East/Central Asia)   1300–1918

Songhay (West Africa)   1400–1590

Aztec (Mexico)   1420–1530

Hapsburg (Europe)   1430–1800

British (Worldwide)   1550–1940

Soviet (Eastern Europe/Central Asia)   1917–1991

*This was the empire of Alexander the Great, the Greek-trained Macedonian warrior who in a very brief time created one of the largest empires ever.

#Genghis Khan was the main leader of this Asiatic empire.

Good Knights!

In olden times, English knights earned their spurs with great deeds on the battlefield. Monarchs chose them and rewarded them with lands and manors and all that cool stuff. Knights today are also chosen by the British monarch, but they are honoured for their work in many areas far from the battlefield. The queen can give honorary knighthoods to folks from elsewhere. (Canadians, such as first prime minister Sir John A. Macdonald, used to be able to accept knighthoods, but that's no longer true.) Here's a list of people awarded honorary knighthoods.

Bono, Irish rock star and activist

George H. W. Bush, former U.S. president

Placido Domingo, Italian opera singer

Terry Matthews*, Canadian business leader

Bob Geldof, Irish musician and fundraiser

Billy Graham, U.S. preacher

Robert Borden, Canadian prime minister

Pelé, Brazilian soccer star

Steven Spielberg, U.S. moviemaker

Donald Tsang, Hong Kong politician

Simon Wiesenthal, Israeli writer

*Canadian business magnate Matthews has done most of his work in Canada . . . but was born in Wales, so *does* get to keep his "Sir."

Knights of the Round Table

Knights often appear in fiction, too. The most famous are the Knights of the Round Table, from the many legends about the British King Arthur. Sir Thomas Malory, a writer in the 1400s, popularized the stories of the Round Table, but parts of them contain much older legends. The knights themselves had many adventures, and while none are as well-known as Arthur, they're still worthy of getting their own list. Here are the main guys who sat around the Round Table. (Some of the names are spelled in different ways in different retellings.)

Sir Bedevere	Sir Galahad	Sir Gereaint	Sir Lancelot
Sir Bors	Sir Gareth	Sir Kay	Sir Percival
Sir Gaheris	Sir Gawain	Sir Lamorak	Sir Tristan

Princess Power!

Though there are dozens of real-life princesses around the world today, they don't wear those pointy hats you see in old paintings, they rarely live in tall towers, and they are never threatened by dragons. However, they are indeed princesses — the daughters of kings and queens or other princes and princesses, or the wives of princes. Only a few belong to royal families that actually rule their countries, but that doesn't mean that every little girl in those countries doesn't look up at the princesses and sigh. . . . Here are few of the world's current princesses.

Belgium
Mathilde, Elisabeth, Astrid, Luisa-Maria, Maria Luisa, Maria Laura, Laetitia Maria, Claire, Louise

Burundi
Esther

Denmark
Mary, Alexandra, Benedikte, Elisabeth

Great Britain
Anne, Beatrice, Eugenie

Japan
Masako, Aiko, Kako, Mako, Hanako, Yuriko, Tonahito, Akiko, Yohko

Liechtenstein
Marie Aglaë, Sophie, Marie-Caroline, Tatjana, Maria-Annunciata, Marie Astrid, Marie Caroline

Luxembourg
Alexandra

Monaco
Caroline, Stéphanie, Charlotte,
Alexandra

Morocco
Lalla Salma, Lalla Asma, Lalla Hasna,
Lalla Meyrem

Netherlands
Máxima, Catharina-Amalia, Alexia,
Laurentien, Mabel

Norway
Mette-Marit, Ingrid Alexandra,
Martha Louise

Romania
Margarita, Sophie, Marie

Russia
Olga

Spain
Letizia, Leonor, Elena, Cristina

Sweden
Victoria, Madeleine

Uganda
Elizabeth

Arrr! Pirates!

Thanks to that guy from the Caribbean, pirates are hot again. For centuries (most famously in the 1500–1700s), they were more than hot — they were starting fires . . . and looting ships and sacking towns and capturing prizes and all that piratical stuff. They were not really nice, after all, and their main job was pretty much breaking every law they could. Some of them gained more fame than others. Here's a list of some real-life (that is, *not* Johnny Depp) pirates.

Blackbeard Perhaps the best-known pirate ever, his real name was Edward Teach. In a wild-and-woolly two-year career, he wrecked dozens of ships and built a reputation for real ferocity.

Anne Bonny Along with her friend Mary Read, Anne was that rarest of people: a female pirate. Sailing on the ship of Calico Jack, she and Jack fought – and went to prison – like other pirates.

Cheng Chiu-Long and Cheng I Sao This pair of Chinese pirates sailed separately, but caused plenty of damage. Cheng I Sao was one of the few female pirate captains.

William Kidd One of the most famous pirates ever, Captain Kidd began his pirating career, like Henry Morgan, with permission to sack enemy ships. He soon moved away from this legal career to a full-blown life as a pirate.

Jean Lafitte This Louisiana-based French pirate turned (temporarily) from criminal to American patriot, helping defeat the British in the Battle of New Orleans during the War of 1812.

Henry Morgan A British captain, he was at first given permission to attack the enemy Spanish . . . but he kept on attacking even after England and Spain made peace!

Black Bart Roberts Another British pirate, he supposedly captured more than 400 ships in his pirating career.

Named for . . .

When French explorer Jacques Cartier sailed up the St. Lawrence River in 1535, the Iroquois introduced their villages as "kanata." Cartier thought that the word referred to the whole area, when it actually just meant "village." By 1550, the whole of the land (or at least what Europeans knew of it, which wasn't much) appeared on maps labelled "Canada." As time went on, some of Canada's provinces and territories were also named after words from Aboriginal languages. Others were named after British royalty.

Newfoundland and Labrador Named "new founde isle" by John Cabot, who landed there in 1497. Labrador means "landholder" in Portuguese

Prince Edward Island Named for Prince Edward, father of Britain's Queen Victoria

Nova Scotia Latin for "New Scotland"

New Brunswick Named after England's King George III, a descendant of the house of Brunswick

Québec Means "narrow passage" in the Algonquin language

Ontario Means "beautiful lake" in the Iroquoian language

Manitoba Means "the strait of the spirit" in the Cree language

Saskatchewan Means "swift-flowing river" in the Cree language

Alberta Named after the Governor General's wife, Princess Louise Caroline Alberta

British Columbia Named after the Columbia River, which was named after American Captain Robert Gray's ship

Yukon Means "great river" in the Athabascan language

Northwest Territories Named for the geographic location of the territory within Canada

Nunavut Means "our land" in Inuktitut

Fathers of . . .

Officially, a man can only be the father of a son or daughter. But that hasn't stopped history from making guys the fathers of all sorts of things. They might have been the inventor or developer of an idea or product, the first leader of a country or a movement, or the person who made something popular. Sir John A. Macdonald is sometimes called the "father of Canadian Confederation," for example. However they got the title, these gents are "Fathers of . . ." the following things.

FATHER	OF
Kemal Ataturk	Turkey*
Stephen Austin	Texas
Alexander Graham Bell	Telephone
Tim Berners-Lee	World Wide Web
Nolan Bushnell	Computer games
Vinton Cerf	The Internet
Louis Daguerre	Photography
Sigmund Freud	Psychoanalysis
Mohandas Gandhi	Modern India
Giuseppe Garabaldi	Modern Italy
Robert Goddard	Rocketry
W.C. Handy	The Blues
Jim Henson	The Muppets
Gugliemo Marconi	Radio
Karl Marx	Communism
Sir John Macdonald	Canadian Federation
Robert Oppenheimer	Atomic bomb
Fr. Junipero Serra	California
Igor Sikorsky	Helicopter
Otto von Bismarck	Modern Germany
John Wanamaker	Department stores

*The nation, not the bird.

Mothers of . . .

Don't worry, we won't leave moms out! Here's a list, similar to the one on page 22, that features women who have gone down in history for being so important to an invention, country, or cause that they are called the "Mother of . . ." But how many of these things do you think send a card on Mother's Day?

MOTHER/OF

Lady Aberdeen/Civil rights

Isadora Duncan/Modern dance

Marguerite Bourgeoys/Montreal

Florence Nightingale/Modern nursing

Dorothy Page/Iditarod dogsled race

Rosa Parks/Civil rights movement

Jeanne Mance/Montreal

Mary Shelley/Science fiction

Winnie Mandela/South Africa

Montreal had two mothers? Well, they actually worked together for many years in the early days of that city. Bourgeoys was a Catholic nun who organized numerous churches and schools. In 1982, she became Canada's first female Catholic saint. Mance, a nurse, was the founder of a hospital in Montreal. Both women played a huge part in making the city.

LOST Civilizations

How can you lose a civilization? You can lose a sock or lose a moment or lose a tooth . . . but a civilization? Well, sadly, it's happened a few times in history. Due to disease or war or drought or just the effects of time, some hearty and healthy civilizations have either disappeared or been swallowed up by others and become just a memory. Plus, there's one on this list that really is just a myth . . . but we thought we'd toss it in here anyway in case you've seen it lying around somewhere.

Anasazi Native American tribe in Southwest U.S. that "vanished" in about 1300.

Angkor Wat Built in the 1100s in what is now Thailand by a now-gone civilization, these temples were lost for hundreds of years before being "found" again in 1860.

Atlantis Mentioned in only a couple of ancient histories, this island nation supposedly sank beneath the waves thousands of years ago.

Babylon A large civilization in Mesopotamia conquered and later abandoned by the Greeks around 312 BCE.

Cahokia/Mississipian At its peak in the 1200s, the Native American city of Cahokia was the biggest in North America; about 200 years later, it was empty.

Pompeii One day in 79, a thriving city-state in Italy. The next, a smoldering heap of ash after Mt. Vesuvius erupted and destroyed the place.

Troy Though there is some disagreement about whether this place was real or not, a site in Turkey is thought by many to have been Troy, site of Homer's *Iliad*, a story about the Trojan War.

World's Fairs

Since the late 1700s, enormous exhibitions called World's Fairs have thrilled millions. The high point of World's Fairs was the three or four decades before World War I. At the Fairs, the host nations put out examples of the many wonderful things in that country. Other countries then constructed large pavilions to do the same. Before the age of air travel and TV, World's Fairs were a great way for people to "see" the world. These days, Fairs are fewer . . . but they're still fun. Here's a list of the last ten World's Fairs, plus a list of some World's Fairs held in North America.

Recent World's Fairs

YEAR	LOCATION
2008	Zaragoza, Spain
2005	Aichi, Japan
2002	Switzerland (several cities)
2000	Hanover, Germany
1998	Lisbon, Portugal
1993	Taejon, South Korea
1992	Genoa, Italy
1992	Seville, Spain
1988	Brisbane, Australia
1986	Vancouver, Canada

World's Fairs in North America Since 1960

1986	Vancouver, B.C.
1984	New Orleans, Louisiana
1982	Knoxville, Tennessee
1974	Spokane, Washington
1968	San Antonio, Texas
1967	Montreal, Quebec
1964	New York, New York
1962	Seattle, Washington

Phamous Pharaohs

In the ancient land of Egypt, the pharaoh was the top cat. Revered as a human god by his (or her) people, pharaohs ruled over Egypt for thousands of years. A few of them stand out from the dusty sands of history as more accomplished or more renowned. Dates shown are the middle of their reigns.

Sneferu, c. 2600 BCE
Built several of the famous pyramids that still stand in Egypt

Khufu, c. 2575 BCE
Builder of the Great Pyramid of Egypt

Khafra, c. 2540 BCE
Erected the famous statue of the Sphinx

Hatshepsut, c. 1490 BCE
An early female pharaoh, she expanded Egypt's trade

Amenhotep III, c. 1375 BCE
Another great builder, he put up several key monuments

Akhenaten, c. 1360 BCE
Tried to get his people to believe in one god instead of many

Tutankhamun, c. 1330 BCE
Not a superstar pharaoh, but his tomb is the best preserved ever found

Ramses II, c. 1250 BCE
Great warrior who defeated the enemy Hittites

Cleopatra, c. 50 BCE
One of only a few female pharaohs

Kids in Charge!

You have to be at least 18 years old to be prime minister of Canada. However, age was no barrier to the kids on this list. They were all (at least in name) the rulers of their countries. Not a bad job if you can get it!

RULER	FIRST YEAR	AGES*
Baldwin V, King of Jerusalem	1177	0–9
Margaret I of Scotland	1283	0–7
Louis XVII of France	1785	0–9
King John I of France	1316	0–5 days
Alfonso XI, King of Leon (in Spain)	1312	1
King Fuad II of Egypt	1952	1
Henry Pu Yi, Emperor of China	1909	3–6
Christina of Sweden	1632	5
Leo II, Byzantine emperor	474	7
James II of Scotland	1437	7
Tutankhamun, Pharaoh of Egypt	1333 BCE	8–18
Edward VI of England	1546	9–16

*Ages in years during time they were in charge, which started in the year listed. Some of them lived longer than their reigns lasted.

$$$ In Your Pocket?

Do you get a weekly allowance? Do you save it or spend it? Take a trip with us on a time machine to 1901. Pretend you live in Toronto, Ontario. Here are some of the things you could spend your allowance on if you shopped at Eaton's. (But don't get too excited — if you were a kid in 1901, you probably wouldn't have gotten an allowance anyway!)

bicycle	$25–$35
football	$1.50–$2.25
harmonica	25¢–75¢
guitar	$4–$20
sled	15¢–$1.25
chess set	35¢–$2.50
skates (blades only)	45¢–$5
Black Beauty (the book)	30¢
boys' pocket watch	$1–$3
hand mirror	20¢–$1.25
doll	10¢–$8.50
dress	59¢–$3.50

MIGHTY Mounties

They're our men and women in red and symbols of our country — they're our Mounties! The Mounties, or Royal Canadian Mounted Police (RCMP) as they are officially known today, were established in 1873 by Prime Minister John A. Macdonald. The Mounties' purpose in those early days was to keep law and order in the Prairies, to curb the lawlessness of the whiskey traders, develop friendly relations with the Native peoples, and pave the way for settlement of the West. As the old saying goes: the Mounties always get their man. Here are stories of a few famous early Mounties.

Colonel James Farquharson MacLeod
led an expedition to capture notorious whiskey-trader troublemakers at Fort Whoop-Up in 1874.

Daniel "Peach" Davis, at 23 years old, led 1,000 displaced
Assiniboine and Cree on a 300-km trek across Saskatchewan in 1882.

Superintendent Sam Steele maintained law and order
during the Klondike Gold Rush in the Yukon in the late 1890s.

Jack Dempster located the bodies of the Mounties of the "Lost
Patrol," who had died after getting lost while delivering mail in 1911.

John Moses was a Special Constable who helped capture the Mad
Trapper of Rat River in 1932 in the Northwest Territories.

The March West

On July 8, 1874, a group of more than 300 Mounties set out from Fort Dufferin, Manitoba, for the West for the very first time. Their wagon train, which included more than 600 animals, stretched for 8 km! They carried guns, food, clothing, building supplies, and even entire field kitchens!

AMERICAN Invasions

One of the main reasons that four provinces joined together to create the Dominion of Canada in 1867 (a.k.a. Confederation) was because they feared invasions from their southern neighbours. And for good reason! From border raids to battles, the Americans had a history of invading Canada. (Don't worry now, though. Today, we're good friends!)

INVASION SITE	YEAR
La Prairie, Quebec	1690
Port Royal, Nova Scotia	1690
Port Royal, Nova Scotia	1704
Port Royal, Nova Scotia	1710
Quebec City, Quebec	1711
Louisbourg, Cape Breton Island, Nova Scotia	1745
Quebec City, Quebec	1775
Queenston, Ontario	1812
Châteauguay River, Quebec	1813
York (Toronto), Ontario	1813
Campobello Island, New Brunswick	1866
Ridgeway, Ontario	1866

Forts IN CANADA

More than 200 forts have been built in Canada. In the east, most forts were built to protect and defend people and land (military forts). In the west, they were built as trading posts, mainly fur-trading forts, or by the North West Mounted Police to maintain law and order during settlement (NWMP forts). Here is a sample of some of the most famous forts from across the land.

NAME	TYPE OF FORT	LOCATION
Cumberland House	fur-trading	Saskatchewan
Fort Battleford	NWMP	Saskatchewan
Fort Edmonton	fur-trading	Alberta
Fort George	military	Ontario
Fort Langley	fur-trading	British Columbia
Fort MacLeod	NWMP	Alberta
Fort Steele	NWMP	British Columbia
Fort York	military	Ontario
Fort William	fur-trading	Ontario
Fortress of Louisbourg	military	Nova Scotia
Lower Fort Garry	fur-trading	Manitoba
Port Royal	military	Nova Scotia
Quebec Citadel	military	Quebec
Signal Hill	military	Newfoundland

Fort Facts!

Fort Whoop-Up, Alberta, did a different kind of trading. It was the root-tootinest whiskey trading fort in the West! Fort Sainte-Marie Among the Hurons in Ontario was the largest mission fort in Canada. Missionaries lived there while they preached Christianity to Aboriginal peoples during early pioneer times.

World War I

From July 1914 to November 1918, the world was at war. Battles between Allied forces (led by Great Britain, France, Canada, and, later, the United States) and forces of the German and Austrian Empires raged in Europe, Asia, Africa, and the Middle East. It was called "the war to end all wars," a statement that has, sadly, proven to be quite false. There's no way to include all the events of the war on this list, but here's a quick overview of some of the most important battles and events.

1914

Aug.: Austria invades Serbia, while Germany invades Luxembourg, Belgium, France, and Prussia. In response, Great Britain, Canada, and Newfoundland join the war to defend allies such as France.

Aug. 30: Battle of Tannenberg; Germany defeats Russian forces advancing on Germany from the east.

Sept.: First Battle of Marne (France) is fought between Allied forces and German troops.

Nov.: First Battle of Ypres (Belgium) is the first real "trench warfare" battle, using what would become the signature strategy of the war.

Nov.: Turkey joins the war on the side of Germany.

1915

Jan. 19: For the first time, German airships, called *Zeppelins*, fly over and bomb England.

April: Germany becomes the first to use poison gas in battle.

May: Second Battle of Ypres. Canadian troops distinguish themselves in this battle, adding to a new and growing sense of national pride.

May 7: Germany sinks the passenger ship *Lusitania*.

1916

Feb.: Battle at Verdun (France).

May: Battle of Jutland between Allied and German naval forces; there is no clear winner.

July–Nov.: The Allied attack becomes the Battle of the Somme in France.

1917

April: A major offensive by Canadian troops at Vimy Ridge drives back German troops. The battle is credited with giving Canada a new spirit of national purpose.

May: Billy Bishop is awarded the Victoria Cross. By the end of the war, he'll have shot down 72 enemy aircraft.

July–Nov.: Third Battle of Ypres, as Allied forces push against German positions. Canadians are a major force in this battle.

1918

July: Germany makes another attack at another Battle of the Marne (France), but can't break through.

Aug.: Australian and Canadian troops drive the Germans back to the Hindenburg Line, their final line of retreat toward Germany.

Nov. 9: Kaiser Wilhelm II of Germany resigns.

Nov. 11: On 11/11/18, at 11 A.M., documents are signed that end the "war to end all wars."

So how did it all start? Well, like most things about wars, it's complicated. However, there was one event that triggered it (or that some countries used as a trigger), and that was when Archduke Franz Ferdinand of Austria was killed on June 28, 1914, in Sarajevo by Gavrilo Princip. The Austrians blamed Serbia (among others) and declared war a few months later. That started the dominos falling and World War I was raging soon after.

World War II

About 20 years after being defeated in World War I, Germany rose up again as a power in Europe. Led by the Nazi dictator Adolf Hitler, Germany invaded neighbouring countries and allied with the equally land-hungry Japanese empire. World War I had been wide-ranging, but World War II was even bigger, with armed battles on almost every continent. Like World War I, it's hard to gather into a list, but we'll give it a try with these key events.

1939

Sept.: Germany invades Poland, and Great Britain and France declare war on Germany to defend Poland. Canada joins a few days later.

1940

Spring: German forces roar through and take over France, Belgium, the Netherlands, Denmark, and Norway.

May: British forces are driven out of Europe at Dunkirk, France, evacuating with help from hundreds of private boats.

July–Sept.: Battle of Britain is fought in the air above England, as British air forces mark a huge victory.

1941

Jan. 21: The battle moves to Africa, as Allied forces battle Germans at Tobruk in Libya.

June 22: Germany invades the Soviet Union; soon after, it takes over Greece and Yugoslavia.

Fall: Japan invades neighbouring countries, including China, the Philippines, and Indonesia.

Dec. 7: Japan bombs U.S. naval base at Pearl Harbor, Hawaii. The U.S. declares war on Japan and Germany.

1942

Spring: Japan continues its march in the Pacific, taking Singapore, Java, Borneo, and Sumatra.

August: A Canadian-led attack force at Dieppe, France, suffers terrible casualties.

Fall: Germany's African forces fall to British troops at the Battle of El Alamein.

1943

Feb.: Soviet forces defeat German forces at Stalingrad in the first major defeat of Germany.

Sept.: Italy is invaded from North Africa by Allied forces, resulting in the surrender of Italy, a key German ally. Canadian forces invade Sicily.

Dec.: Canadian forces retake the town of Ortona, Italy from the Germans.

1944

June 5: A month after a major invasion at Anzio, Italy, Rome is recaptured from German forces by Allied armies.

June 6: D-Day, the invasion of German-controlled Europe by Allied forces. The area known as Juno Beach is the responsibility of Canadian forces.

Aug.: Paris is freed of German control for the first time since 1940.

Dec.: The Battle of the Bulge is fought as Germany tries to counterattack.

1945

Jan.: Allied forces retake the Philippines.

Spring: German V1 and V2 rocket bombs continue to land in England.

April 21: After a race through Germany by the Allied and Soviet armies, Soviet forces are the first to reach the German capital of Berlin.

May 7: Germany surrenders; Hitler commits suicide.

Aug.: U.S. plane drops atomic bombs on Hiroshima and Nagasaki, Japan, the first (and still only) used in combat.

Aug. 14: Japan surrenders.

PM Runners-Up

We all know Canada's prime ministers by heart, right? But how about the Opposition leaders? The leader of the Opposition is the head of the party that wins the second-most seats in a federal election. They lost, but they did win the right to yell at the P.M. during question period! How many of these Opposition leaders do you recognize? (We've listed the prime ministers below, too — bonus information!)

LEADER OF THE OFFICIAL OPPOSITION	ELECTION YEAR	P.M.
Stéphane Dion (Liberal)	2008	Stephen Harper
Bill Graham (Liberal)	2006	Stephen Harper
Stephen Harper (Can. Alliance)	2004	Paul Martin
Stockwell Day (Can. Alliance)	2000	Jean Chrétien
Preston Manning (Reform)	1997	Jean Chrétien
Lucien Bouchard (Bloc Québécois)	1993	Jean Chrétien
John Turner (Liberal)	1988	Brian Mulroney
John Turner (Liberal)	1984	Brian Mulroney
Joseph Clark (PC)	1980	Pierre Elliot Trudeau
Pierre E. Trudeau (Liberal)	1979	Joseph Clark
Robert Stanfield (PC)	1974	Pierre Elliot Trudeau
Robert Stanfield (PC)	1972	Pierre Elliot Trudeau
Robert Stanfield (PC)	1968	Pierre Elliot Trudeau
John Diefenbaker (PC)	1965	Lester B. Pearson
John Diefenbaker (PC)	1963	Lester B. Pearson
Lester B. Pearson (Liberal)	1962	John Diefenbaker
Lester B. Pearson (Liberal)	1958	John Diefenbaker

LEADER OF THE OFFICIAL OPPOSITION	ELECTION YEAR	P.M.
Louis St-Laurent (Liberal)	1957	John Diefenbaker
George Drew (PC)	1953	Louis St-Laurent
George Drew (PC)	1949	Louis St-Laurent
John Bracken (PC)	1945	W.L. Mackenzie King
Richard Hanson (Conservative)	1940	W.L. Mackenzie King
R.B. Bennett (Conservative)	1935	W.L. Mackenzie King
W.L. Mackenzie King (Liberal)	1930	R.B. Bennett
Hugh Guthrie (Conservative)	1926	W.L. Mackenzie King
Arthur Meighen (Conservative)	1925	W.L. Mackenzie King
Arthur Meighen (Conservative)	1921	W.L. Mackenzie King
Wilfrid Laurier (Liberal)	1917	Robert Borden
Wilfrid Laurier (Liberal)	1911	Robert Borden
Robert Borden (Conservative)	1908	Wilfrid Laurier
Robert Borden (Conservative)	1904	Wilfrid Laurier
Robert Borden (Conservative)	1900	Wilfrid Laurier
Charles Tupper (Conservative)	1896	Wilfrid Laurier
Wilfrid Laurier (Liberal)	1891	John A. Macdonald
Edward Blake (Liberal)	1887	John A. Macdonald
Edward Blake (Liberal)	1882	John A. Macdonald
Alexander Mackenzie (Liberal)	1878	John A. Macdonald
John A. Macdonald (Conservative)	1874	Alexander Mackenzie
Alexander Mackenzie (Liberal)	1872	John A. Macdonald
Edward Blake (Liberal)	1867	John A. Macdonald

Gearin' Up

A Bicycle Timeline

Cavemen didn't have 'em, Socrates never saw one, Columbus didn't ride one, and Samuel de Champlain was stuck with a canoe. What were they all missing out on? Bicycles! Here's a quick rundown on how the modern bicycle was developed.

1817 Germany's Karl Drais created a two-wheeled contraption that a person could "ride" by sitting on it and just walking.

1860s The "boneshaker" became a hit. The model made by Pierre Michaux of France was popular; it had spinning pedals that turned the hard wheels directly, without a chain.

1870 James Starley created the penny farthing, a bike with an enormous front wheel. The rider sat as much as 2.4 m (8 ft.) above the ground!

1885 Starley's nephew John created the Rover, a bike that looked much more like today's. Its diamond-shaped frame featured a chain, pedals, a more comfortable seat, and handlebars. This became known as the "safety bike" model.

1888 Inflatable tires were first used; whew! Before then, tires were solid, so you can imagine that the ride was not too smooth!

1890s Invention of coaster brakes, hand brakes, and gears. Before then: no brakes . . . no gears!

1970 First BMX bike track opened in California.

1979 Gary Fisher started the first "mountain bike" company, creating a whole new class of bikes.

Revvin' Up
An Automobile Timeline

It's hard to believe, but less than a century ago, more people got around on horses than in cars. Today, of course, there are about as many cars in the North America as there are people, and there's almost no place on the planet you can go without having to look both ways before you cross the street. Where did they all come from? Here are some key milestones in the early history of automobiles. Start your engines!

1862 Étienne Lenoir of France created the first gasoline engine. He tried it on a wagon (after unhitching the horse, of course) and went 19 km (12 miles). Then he forgot all about it and worked on motorboats.

1876 German engineer Nicholas Otto created a type of gasoline engine known as a "four-stroke." It became the model for all future engines.

1885 Karl Benz (yep, the future Mercedes-Benz guy) was the first person to combine a gas engine with a frame and wheels to make . . . ta-dah! . . . a motor car.

1891 Charles Duryea made the first cars in America. Eight years later, Random Olds (later of "Oldsmobile" fame) opened the first car factory in America.

1907 McLaughlin Motor Car Company opened in Oshawa, Ontario.

1908 Henry Ford introduced the Model T, the first mass-produced car.

1937 The first versions of the Volkswagen Beetle hit the road in Germany; it became one of the world's bestselling car models, with more than 21 million sold.

1957 Japanese cars (Toyotas) entered the American market.

1997 In Japan, the Toyota Prius became the first mass-produced gas-electric hybrid car.

FOLLOW IN HER Footsteps

Are you the kind of girl who dreams of the thrill of an election debate, or of being in the spotlight of a scrum on Parliament Hill? If so, you have these Canadian women to thank.

The first woman in Canadian politics to be . . .

a Member of Parliament,
Agnes Macphail, 1921

a senator,
Cairine Wilson, 1930

mayor of a major Canadian city,
Charlotte Whitton
(in Ottawa), 1951

a federal Cabinet minister,
Ellen Fairclough
(Minister of Citizenship and Immigration), 1957

an ambassador,
Margaret Meagher
(to Israel), 1958

appointed to the
Supreme Court of Canada,
   Bertha Wilson, 1982

Governor General,
   Jeanne Sauvé, 1984

leader of a federal party,
   Audrey McLaughlin
   (NDP), 1989

a provincial premier,
   Rita Johnston
   (in British Columbia), 1991

prime minister,
   Kim Campbell, 1993

chief justice of the Supreme Court,
   Beverley McLachlin, 1999

Who got the Vote?

The Canada Elections Act of 1918 gave all Canadian women over 21 the right to vote federally. But in provincial elections, this right was granted by the province. The first were Alberta, Manitoba, and Saskatchewan in 1916. The last was Quebec in 1940.

Then vs. Now

(or One Hundred Years Later)

PROVINCE/TERRITORY

Prince Edward Island

Nova Scotia

New Brunswick

Quebec

Ontario

Manitoba

Saskatchewan

Alberta

British Columbia

Yukon

Northwest Territories

At the turn of the last century, Canada was a much different place than it is today. The entire population in 1901 was just 5,371,315 people. One hundred years later, it was 30,007,000! That's about 5.5 times more people. As you look at this list, you might wonder where Nunavut and Newfoundland are. Well, Nunavut's numbers in 1901 are tied in with the Northwest Territories. It became a separate territory in 1999. Newfoundland and Labrador was a British colony until 1949.

POPULATION		INCREASE OF
1901	2001	
103,259	135,294	1.3%
459,574	908,007	2%
331,120	729,498	2.2%
1,648,898	7,237,479	4.4%
2,182,947	11,410,046	5.2%
255,211	1,119,583	4.4%
91,279	978,933	10.7%
73,022	2,974,807	40.7%
178,657	3,907,738	21.9%
27,219	28,674	1%
20,129	37,360	1.9%

History
Game Page

We'll start you off with a two-part game. First, fill in the missing years in the questions. Then find the answers in the grid at the bottom. They'll be in the grid vertically or horizontally, not diagonally, but they might be backward or upside-down! The answers to the questions should be found in this History chapter.

1. In what year did World War I end? _____

2. The most recent North American World's Fair was in _____.

3. When did the Devonian age begin? _____

4. In what year was Pierre Trudeau leader of the Opposition? _____

5. When did John Cabot land in Canada? _____

6. In what year did the Mounties capture the Mad Trapper of Rat River? _____

7. When did the battle at Vimy Ridge happen? _____

8. When did the first BMX bike track open? _____

9. When did John Turner start his second term as Opposition leader? _____

10. In what year was the D-Day invasion? _____

1	1	9	8	7	4	0	7	1	1	3	4
2	3	9	1	3	2	8	5	9	1	0	1
8	1	4	9	7	0	4	2	1	7	1	9
9	8	7	4	5	1	2	3	7	9	8	1
1	8	9	4	0	9	6	6	0	1	9	8
1	9	4	4	7	9	2	0	1	4	3	0
9	1	4	5	8	0	9	6	1	9	3	2
7	4	0	3	5	8	1	9	7	9	2	9
0	6	8	9	1	8	3	6	5	0	1	0

CHAPTER TWO

Social Studies

Go to outer space, be prime minister, live in a castle, visit a national landmark, or have more money than anyone else in the world. Can't do all that? No problem. Just read this chapter and do all that and more.

Canada's Islands

Canada's motto is "from sea to sea," which includes most of the land north of the 49th parallel (and a fair bit south of it, too) from the Atlantic Ocean in the east to the Pacific Ocean in the west. Canada also claims land that lies beyond the coasts — over 52,000 sea islands. Here are just a few notable islands.

Largest island: **Baffin Island**

Largest island with
a permanent fixed link to the mainland:
Cape Breton Island

Only island province:
Prince Edward Island

Most populated island: **Vancouver Island**

Northernmost island: **Ellesmere Island**

Least densely populated island:
Ellesmere Island

Most densely populated island:
Prince Edward Island

Island inhabited by wild horses:
Sable Island

Island with the highest number
of resident artists: **Hornby Island**

Largest uninhabited island: **Devon Island**

Honouring OUR BEST

Just like the awards you get from your school, the Canadian government has a way of recognizing Canada's best. Canada's top honours are presented by the governor general on behalf of all Canadians. Here is a list of the national honours that you, too, may some day receive at a special ceremony at Rideau Hall. (Here's some advice: dress up — you'll need somewhere nice to pin your shiny new medal!)

The Order of Canada

Recognizes a lifetime of outstanding achievement, dedication to the community and service to the nation.

Order of Military Merit

For exceptional service in the Canadian Forces and dedication and devotion beyond the call of duty.

Order of Merit of the Police Forces

This goes to members of the police service for careers of exceptional merit, contributions to policing and community development.

Royal Victorian Order

Awarded to those who perform special or extraordinary service to a member of the royal family.

Most Venerable Order of the Hospital of St. John of Jerusalem

This honour goes to members of the humanitarian organization the Order of St. John, for the amount and quality of charitable work they have performed.

The governor general also gives awards to signify excellence in the arts: the Governor General's Awards in Visual and Media Arts, the Governor General's Medals in Architecture, and our favourites — the Governor General's Literary Awards. (Do you think we've got a chance?)

Island Countries

An island is a landform that is completely surrounded by water. There are hundreds of thousands of islands around the world, but only these 44 are independent countries. Let's hope all their inhabitants know how to swim . . . .

Antigua and Barbuda
Australia
Bahamas
Bahrain
Barbados
Cape Verde
Comoros
Cuba
Cyprus
Dominica
East Timor

Fiji
Grenada
Iceland
Indonesia
Ireland
Jamaica
Japan
Kiribati
Madagascar
Maldives
Malta
Marshall Islands
Mauritius
Micronesia
Nauru
New Zealand
Palau

The Philippines
St. Kitts and Nevis
St. Lucia
St. Vincent and the Grenadines
Samoa
São Tomé and Príncipe
Seychelles
Singapore
Solomon Islands
Sri Lanka
Taiwan
Tonga
Trinidad and Tobago
Tuvalu
United Kingdom
Vanuatu

Own Your Own Island

Perhaps the title of this list should be "Have Lots of Money and Own Your Own Island." With enough money, you can own an island in its wild, natural state or an island ready to be filled with buildings and people. Have fun shopping!

ISLAND	LOCATION	COST (in millions)
James Island	Canada	$49
Isla de sa Ferradura	Spain	$39
Keswick Island	Australia	$33
Koro Island	Fiji	$27.5
Sultan's Island	Indonesia	$27.5
Blue Lagoon Island	Fiji	$25
Isle of St. John	USA	$25
Koh Fan Noi and Koh Fan Yai	Thailand	$24
Little Ragged Island	Bahamas	$24
Thatch Cay	St. Thomas	$24
Haapiti Nui Island	French Polynesia	$18

Got Island?

Believe it or not, it's pretty easy to find an island to buy (if you've got the money!). Several companies represent people trying to buy and sell islands. One Web site has a quiz you can take to see if island living is for you. One question asks what you like to do on vacation . . . another asks what you would do if your toilet overflowed!

Famous Castles

Castles bring up images of knights, drawbridges, and battles, but many castles are just home sweet home. They are called castles because of their size and architecture. This list of world castles includes both military castles and castle homes. You can visit many of them, such as Bran Castle (legendary home of Count Dracula) and Neuschwanstein (the model for many fairy-tale castles).

CASTLE	COUNTRY
Alhambra	Spain
Amber Fort	India
Blair Castle	Scotland
Blarney Castle	Ireland
Bran Castle	Romania
Cardiff Castle	Wales
Casa Loma	Canada
Castel del Monte	Italy
Edinburgh Castle	Scotland
Le Mont St. Michel	France
Kremlin	Russia
Laquila Castle	Italy
Heidelberg Castle	Germany
Himeji Castle	Japan
Gondar Castles	Ethiopia
Mysore Palace	India
Neuschwanstein	Germany
Nijo Castle	Japan
Red Fort	India
Tower of London	England
Versailles	France
Windsor Castle	England

They've Struck Oil

Oil: The whole world needs it to do everything from power cars to heat homes, but not every country has its own supply. The future of energy may include greater use of solar, wind, and nuclear power, but until those are more developed, here are the places the world will look to get the oil it needs.

COUNTRY/OIL RESERVES (billion barrels)

Saudi Arabia/**262**

Canada/**179**

Iran/**126**

Iraq/**115**

Kuwait/**102**

United Arab Emirates/**98**

Venezuela/**77**

Russia/**60**

Libya/**39**

Nigeria/**35**

? Oil is measured in barrels, not gallons. How much oil is in one barrel? Most experts use a standard of 158 l (42 gallons) to equal one barrel (though, to make matters more confusing, the standard barrel used to ship oil holds 208 l/55 gallons). One barrel of oil is the same as 224 cans of pop. Two million barrels of oil (or so) would fill a football stadium.

WORLD'S BUSIEST
Airports

Someone really does count the passengers flying in and out of airports! This list includes the airports that have the most passengers going through them each year, listed in order of busiest. Also, the list shows the home city and three-letter code that is used around the world for each airport; learn the secret language of airlines!

Hartsfield-Jackson Atlanta International Airport
(ATL) Atlanta, Georgia

O'Hare International Airport
(ORD) Chicago, Illinois

Heathrow Airport
(LHR) London, England

Haneda Airport
(HND) Tokyo, Japan

Los Angeles International Airport
(LAX) Los Angeles, California

Dallas/Fort Worth International Airport
(DFW) Dallas, Texas

Charles de Gaulle Airport
(CDG) Paris, France

Frankfurt Airport
(FRA) Frankfurt, Germany

Beijing Airport
(PHX) Beijing, China

Denver International Airport
(DEN) Denver, Colorado

McCarran International Airport
(LAS) Las Vegas, Nevada

Amsterdam Airport Schiphol
(AMS) Amsterdam, Netherlands

CITIES WITH
Subways

Subway cars chug through tunnels beneath more than 90 cities around the world. London has the oldest subway, opened in 1863. Boston was the first city in the United States to have a subway system, in 1898. The first subway in Canada opened in Toronto in 1954.

Subways (or Light Rail) in Canada

Calgary

Edmonton

Montreal

Toronto

Vancouver

Busiest Subways Around the World

Moscow	Paris
Tokyo	Osaka
Seoul	London
Mexico City	Hong Kong
New York City	St. Petersburg

Cleveland, Ohio, began building a subway system in 1920 and finally stopped construction in 1948 — without finishing it. Many of the stations and tunnels still exist under the city, but the system never opened.

SPENDING OUR Money

You might have heard your parents grumbling each spring during tax season. This is because their yearly personal income tax is due on April 30. In 2007, the federal government collected $236 billion from Canadians in taxes and other revenues. Where does all the tax money that the government collects go? Canada uses that money in thousands of ways, big and small — from running the military to helping those in need. If you were take one loonie of the tax money they paid and divide it up by how the government spends it, here's what it would look like. (Note: It doesn't add to 100 percent due to the rounding off of some numbers.)

GOVERNMENT SPENDING   **PART OF YOUR LOONIE**

Payments to people   23.5¢

This money goes to look after people, such as money for the elderly, people who are unemployed, and families with young children.

Payments to provinces and territories   19.5¢

This is money for the provinces and territories to use for things such as health care, education, and social programs.

Interest payments   14.5¢

That's interest the government has to pay on money it borrowed.

Payments to individuals, governments, and other organizations and agencies 11¢

Includes money for Aboriginal peoples, farmers, health research, and funding for arts, sports, and multiculturalism.

Federal departments and agencies 11¢

This money goes to support the different government departments that look after things important to Canadians, such as the environment, fisheries and oceans, industry, national resources, public works, veterans, and agencies such as Parks Canada.

Public Safety, Canada Revenue Agency, Crown Corporations 9¢

These "cents" to go the Mounties, prisons, and border operations; the agency that collects taxes; and to a wide variety of businesses owned by the government, including the CBC, museums, and Atomic Energy of Canada.

Department of National Defence 7¢

This provides funding to support Canada's military.

PLUS: Budget Surplus 6¢

This is money that is left over. But we don't get to keep it, the money goes towards paying down the federal debt, which is about $467 billion.

Cabinet Full o'
Ministers

There are about 30 different departments within the Canadian government. The leader of each department is called a minister. Ministers make decisions and answer questions about their department. These ministers are chosen by the prime minister and make up his Cabinet. They need a big table to hold meetings — these are just some of the jobs Canadian Cabinet ministers currently hold.

Minister of . . .

Agriculture and Agri-Food
Canadian Heritage and Official Languages
Citizenship, Immigration, and Multiculturalism
Environment
Finance
Fisheries and Oceans
Foreign Affairs
Health
Human Resources and Skills Development
Indian Affairs and Northern Development
Industry
International Trade
Justice
Labour
National Defence
National Revenue
Natural Resources
Public Safety
Public Works and Government Service
Transport, Infrastructure, and Communities
Veterans Affairs

Stick Around

How long we will live is determined by many factors — some we can control and some we can't. The country in which you live is one of the most important factors. Swaziland has the lowest life expectancy (the number of years most people can be expected to live, based on the average of all the people in the country), at 33.2 years. Life expectancy in Canada is a robust 80.4 years. These 15 countries have the highest life expectancies.

COUNTRY	LIFE EXPECTANCY (YRS.)
Andorra	83.5
San Marino	81.6
Singapore	81.6
Japan	81.2
Australia	80.4
Canada	80.4
Sweden	80.4
Switzerland	80.4
Iceland	80.2
Italy	79.7
France	79.6
Liechtenstein	79.5
Monaco	79.5
Spain	79.5
Norway	79.4

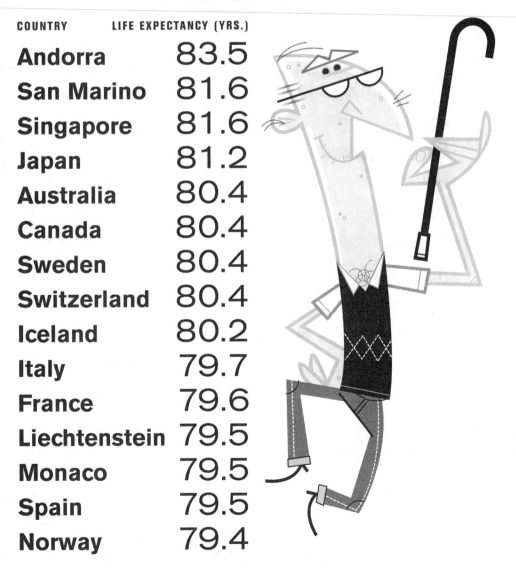

Joining
The Nation

How do you celebrate Canada's birthday? With fireworks, corn roasts, camping, or parades? We mark this event each year with Canada Day on July 1. Canada was first organized into four provinces on July 1, 1867. Today's list of ten provinces and three territories was completed on April 1, 1999 (and that's no April Fool's Day joke). When did your province or territory become a part of Canada?

PROVINCE	JOINED CONFEDERATION ON . . .
British Columbia	July 20, 1871
Alberta	September 1, 1905
Saskatchewan	September 1, 1905
Manitoba	July 15, 1870
Ontario	July 1, 1867
Quebec	July 1, 1867
New Brunswick	July 1, 1867
Nova Scotia	July 1, 1867
Prince Edward Island	July 1, 1873
Newfoundland and Labrador	March 31, 1949

TERRITORY	CREATED ON . . .
Yukon	June 13, 1898
Northwest Territories	July 15, 1870
Nunavut	April 1, 1999

Politics
and other professions

What does it take to be a political leader in this country? Most provincial premiers started their careers as lawyers, civil servants, physicians, teachers, or newspaper editors. Here is a list of some of the more interesting jobs they've held.

Harlan Carey Brewster (British Columbia)
ship's purser, salmon canner

Ujjal Dosanjh (British Columbia): civil rights activist

Tommy Douglas (Saskatchewan): Baptist minister

Donald R. Getty (Alberta): pro football player

Roger Grimes (Newfoundland and Labrador): union leader

Mike Harris (Ontario): golf course manager

James M. Lee (Prince Edward Island): real estate agent

René Lévesque (Quebec): journalist

Rodney MacDonald (Nova Scotia): fiddler, gym teacher

Frank Miller (Ontario)
car salesman, chemical engineer

Keith Milligan (Prince Edward Island)
elk and silver fox farmer

John Norquay (Manitoba): fur trader

Tobias Crawford Norris (Manitoba): auctioneer

Charles Augustus Semlin (British Columbia):
gold prospector

Simon Fraser Tolmie (British Columbia): veterinarian

Walter C. Weir (Manitoba): mortician

PM Facts

We're not talking about stuff you learn in the afternoon . . . we're talking about your prime minister. How well do you know the prime ministers of Canada? Here are some little known facts about some of them.

The first prime minster to die while still in office was **Sir John A. Macdonald**, who also just happened to be our first prime minister.

Sir John C. Abbott was the first prime minster to be born in Canada – in what is now Saint-André-Est, Quebec (but was then St. Andrew, Lower Canada).

The first French-Canadian prime minster was **Sir Wilfrid Laurier**.

Alexander Mackenzie is the only early PM without the title "sir" before his name. That's because he refused a knighthood at a time when all Canadian prime ministers were knighted.

The first Catholic prime minister was **Sir John Sparrow David Thompson**.

The first prime minister to be forced from office by his cabinet was **Sir Mackenzie Bowell**, which prompted him to name-call them "a nest of traitors."

First prime minister to remain a bachelor was **William Lyon Mackenzie King**.

William Lyon Mackenzie King was also a "spiritualist," who held séances through which he received advice on governing the country from the dead.

The only prime minister who is not buried in Canada is **R.B. Bennett**. His final resting place is in England.

The first prime minister to live at 24 Sussex was **Louis St-Laurent**.

The 13th prime minister, **John Diefenbaker**, met the 7th prime minister, Sir Wilfrid Laurier, when he was just 14 years old and working as a newspaper boy at a Saskatoon railway station. "Well, Mr. Prime Minister, I can't waste any more time on you. I must get back to work," he reportedly told the PM.

John Diefenbaker had a top-secret cold war bunker built outside of Ottawa in case of a nuclear attack during the Cold War. It is now called the "Diefenbunker."

The first prime minister to win the Nobel Peace Prize was **Lester B. Pearson**.

As a young man, **Pierre Trudeau** was arrested in Jordan on suspicion of being an Israeli spy!

The first female prime minister was **Kim Campbell**.

The 18th prime minister, **Brian Mulroney**, was a student advisor to the 13th prime minister, John Diefenbaker.

The 20th prime minister, **Jean Chrétien**, shared a birthday with the first prime minister, Sir John A. Macdonald (though Sir John A. thought his birthday was on Jan 10).

The Supremes

Canada's top court is the Supreme Court of Canada, which meets in Ottawa. The nine judges of this court, appointed by the governor general, on advice from the prime minister and his cabinet, help interpret laws and hear appeals from provincial and territorial courts. Once a Supreme Court judge has been appointed, he or she can keep the job until the retirement age of 75 years old. Canada's longest serving Supreme Court judge was Lyman Poore Duff, who served for 37 years. Here are today's Supreme Court judges.

JUSTICE	BEGAN SERVICE
Beverley McLachlin	March 30, 1989
William Ian Corneil Binnie	January 8, 1998
Louis LeBel	January 7, 2000
Marie Deschamps	August 7, 2002
Morris J. Fish	August 5, 2003
Louise Charron	August 30, 2004
Rosalie Silberman Abella	August 30, 2004
Marshall Rothstein	March 1, 2006
Thomas Cromwell	January 5, 2009

Where do they hang their robes? The judges come from across the country, but must live within 40 km of the capital region while they serve the Court. By law, three of the judges are from Quebec. Other judges come from Ontario (three judges), Western Canada (two judges) and Atlantic Canada (one judge).

Canadians In Space

Space is one big place . . . and Canadians are among the many people exploring that vast, well . . . space. The Canadian Space Agency (CSA) is based out of Saint-Hubert, Quebec. One of its most important contributions to space exploration so far has been the Canadarm and the Canadarm 2. Another important contribution is its astronauts. Let's meet some of them! (*STS stands for Shuttle Transport System; these are all space shuttle missions sent up by NASA on which CSA astronauts flew.)

CHRIS HADFIELD

ASTRONAUT SINCE: 1992

MISSIONS: Mission Specialist 1 on missions STS-74 and STS-100

JULIE PAYETTE

ASTRONAUT SINCE: 1992

MISSIONS: Crewmember of mission STS-96, crewmember of upcoming mission STS-127, ISS Assembly Mission 2J/A in 2009

BJARNI TRYGGVASON

ASTRONAUT SINCE: 1983

MISSIONS: Payload Specialist on mission STS-85

DAVE WILLIAMS

ASTRONAUT SINCE: 1992 (now retired)

MISSIONS: Mission Specialist 3 on mission STS-90, NEEMO 1 and NEEMO 9 missions (underwater), and Mission Specialist on mission STS-118

Statues on
Parliament Hill

Next time you visit Parliament Hill in Ottawa on a field trip or family holiday, take the time to see if you can find the statues of these famous people who played a part in Canadian history.

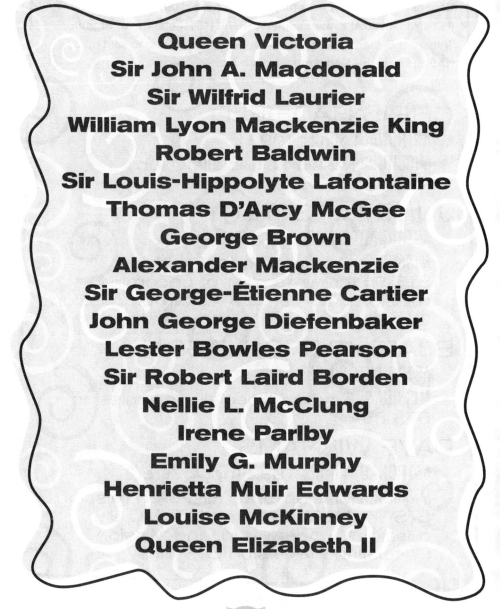

Queen Victoria
Sir John A. Macdonald
Sir Wilfrid Laurier
William Lyon Mackenzie King
Robert Baldwin
Sir Louis-Hippolyte Lafontaine
Thomas D'Arcy McGee
George Brown
Alexander Mackenzie
Sir George-Étienne Cartier
John George Diefenbaker
Lester Bowles Pearson
Sir Robert Laird Borden
Nellie L. McClung
Irene Parlby
Emily G. Murphy
Henrietta Muir Edwards
Louise McKinney
Queen Elizabeth II

ODD Landmarks

In *Scholastic Canada Book of Lists*, we gave you a list of some big Canadian landmarks. Well, here's another list of "big" Canadian landmarks. This list is a little different than in the first book because, well . . . you'll see.

LANDMARK	LOCATION
Big apple	Colborne, ON
Big Atlantic salmon	Campbellton, NB
Big beaver	Grande Prairie, AB
Big Canada goose	Wawa, ON
Big catfish	Selkirk, MB
Big grasshopper	Wilkie, SK
Big groundhog	Wiarton, ON
Big moose	Moose Jaw, SK
Big orange	Montreal, QC
Big potato	O'Leary, PE
Big pysanka*	Vegreville, AB
Big T-rex	Drumheller, AB
Big teepee	Medicine Hat, AB
Big tomato	Leamington, ON
Big woolly mammoth	Kyle, SK

* A Ukrainian Easter egg, of course!

Royal Roll Call

When we think about royalty, we usually think of "Once upon a time . . ."
But kings, queens, sultans, emperors, sheiks, princes, and emirs still rule in
some countries. Some of these royals have absolute power in their countries.
Other kings and queens hold positions in constitutional governments.

COUNTRY	MONARCH (AS OF THE END OF 2008)
Bahrain	King Hamad bin Isa al-Khalifa
Belgium	King Albert II
Bhutan	King Jigme Khesar Namgyel Wangchuck
Brunei	Sultan Haji Hassanal Bolkiah
Cambodia	King Norodom Sihamoni
Denmark	Queen Margrethe II
Japan	Emperor Akihito
Jordan	King Abdallah II
Kuwait	Amir Sabah al-Ahmad al-Jiber al-Sabah
Lesotho	King Letsie III
Liechtenstein	Prince Hans Adam II
Luxembourg	Grand Duke Henri
Malaysia	Sultan Mizan Zainal Abidin
Monaco	Prince Albert II
Morocco	King Mahammed VI
Netherlands	Queen Beatrix
Norway	King Harald V
Oman	Sultan Qaboos bin Said al-Said
Qatar	Amir Hamad bin Khalifa al-Thani
Saudi Arabia	King Abdallah bin Abd al-Aziz Al Saud
Spain	King Juan Carlos I
Swaziland	King Mswati III
Sweden	King Carl XVI Gustaf
Tonga	King George Tupou V
United Kingdom	Queen Elizabeth II

Are You on This List?

Have you ever noticed that there seem to be a lot of people with the same name in your school, or even in your class? If you went back in time about 50 years ago, you'd find that there are lot of kids then with the same name, too, but those names would be much different than today's!

Most popular kids' names in Canada today

GIRLS	BOYS
Emma	Mathew
Emily	Jacob
Sarah	Ethan
Olivia	Alexander
Madison	Nathan
Hannah	William
Megan	Nicolas
Abigail	Joshua
Chloe	Zack
Haley	Samuel
Jessica	Ryan
Julia	Noah

Most popular kids' names of the 1950s

GIRLS	BOYS
Mary	Michael
Linda	James
Deborah	Robert
Patricia	John
Susan	David
Debra	William
Barbara	Richard
Karen	Thomas
Nancy	Gary
Cynthia	Charles
Donna	Steven
Pamela	Mark

Rich People

We wish you the best of luck in someday finding your name on this list (put together in 2008 by the money-obsessed people at *Forbes* magazine). And remember that you were inspired to earn your place by reading this book. You can send your thanks to us in the form of a large cheque! Thank you.
P.S. Just kidding!

Top 10 Richest People in the World

		WEALTH (IN U.S. BILLIONS)	COUNTRY
1.	Warren Buffett	$62	USA
2.	Carlos Slim Helú	$60	Mexico
3.	Bill Gates	$58	USA
4.	Lakshmi Mittal	$45	India
5.	Mukesh Ambani	$43	India
6.	Anil Ambani	$42	India
7.	Ingvar Kamprad	$31	Switzerland
8.	KP Singh	$30	India
9.	Oleg Deripaska	$28	Russia
10.	Karl Albrecht	$27	Germany

Top 10 Richest Canadians (Canadian Business)

		WEALTH (IN CANADIAN BILLIONS)	CITY
1.	Thomson Family	$18.45	Toronto
2.	Irving Brothers	$7.1	Saint John
3.	Galen Weston	$6.6	Toronto
4.	Ted Rogers	$5.05	Toronto
5.	James Pattison	$4.9	Vancouver
6.	Alex Schnaider	$4.25	Toronto
7.	David Azrieli	$4.1	Montreal
8.	Paul Desmarais Sr.	$4.1	Montreal
9.	Bernard Sherman	$3.8	Toronto
10.	Jeff Skoll	$3.1	California

Rich Places

With the exception of Antarctica, billionaires live on every continent, in more than 50 countries. These are the top 20; is your favourite country on this list?

COUNTRY	NUMBER OF BILLIONAIRES
United States	371
Germany	55
Russia	33
Japan	27
United Kingdom	24
India	23
Canada	22
Turkey	21
Hong Kong	17
Brazil	16
France	14
Italy	14
Saudi Arabia	11
Mexico	10
Spain	10
China	8
Malaysia	8
Sweden	8
Switzerland	8
Israel	8

Famous Places

Most people think they can pray — if they pray — anywhere at all. However, the major faiths around the world have special places where people of those faiths gather together to worship. This list consists of some of the most famous places of worship around the world for the major world religions. Many are open to the public, so if you're in their area, look 'em up!

PLACE OF WORSHIP	LOCATION	FAITH
Al-Aqsa Mosque	Jerusalem, Israel	Islam
Laxminarayan Temple	Delhi, India	Hinduism
Al Rashide Mosque	Edmonton, Alberta	Islam
Bahá'í House of Worship	New Delhi, India	Bahá'í
Basilica of Guadalupe	Mexico City, Mexico	Roman Catholic
Basilica of Notre Dame	Montreal, Quebec	Roman Catholic
Canterbury Cathedral	Canterbury, England	Anglican
Cathedral of St. Basil the Blessed	Moscow, Russia	Russian Orthodox
Cologne Cathedral	Cologne, Germany	Roman Catholic
Crystal Cathedral	Garden Grove, Calif.	Protestant
Haeinsa Temple	Gayasan Mt., S. Korea	Buddhism
Harmandir Sahib– Golden Temple	Amritsar, India	Sikhism

# of Worship

PLACE OF WORSHIP	LOCATION	FAITH
Holy Temple, Beit HaMikdash	Jerusalem, Israel	Judaism
Itsukushima Shrine	Miyajima, Japan	Shinto
Great Mosque & Kaaba	Mecca, Saudi Arabia	Islam
Masjid al-Nabawi	Medina, Saudi Arabia	Islam
Meiji Shrine	Tokyo, Japan	Shinto
Salt Lake Tabernacle	Salt Lake City, Utah	Mormon
Notre-Dame de Paris	Paris, France	Roman Catholic
St. Patrick's Cathedral	New York City	Roman Catholic
St. Peter's Cathedral	Vatican City	Roman Catholic
Temple of Saint Sava	Belgrade, Serbia	Eastern Orthodox
Touro Synagogue	Newport, R.I.	Judaism
Washington National Cathedral	Washington, D.C.	Episcopal
Wat Phra Chatuphon	Bangkok, Thailand	Buddhism
Westminster Abbey	London, England	Anglican

Who is buried in Westminster Abbey? Under its stone floors, a favourite tourist spot, are people such as Isaac Newton, Charles Darwin, Geoffrey Chaucer, Charles Dickens, and Laurence Olivier.

Don't Do This in . . .

There's an old saying that goes "When in Rome, do as the Romans do." It means that you should respect the cultures and ways of the native people when you visit foreign lands. Things that we do here might be very offensive to people in other places, while things they expect us to do might be the last thing we think of! Here's a quick introduction to the kinds of things to consider when visiting other countries.

Most Arab countries

✘ Don't point or eat with your left hand; it is considered unclean.

✘ The thumbs-up hand motion doesn't mean "Way to go!" It's actually an insult.

China

✘ Men should never touch women in public.

✘ Avoid using big hand gestures when you talk.

✘ The number four is considered very unlucky here.

Germany

✘ Don't be late to meet someone. German people are very punctual and being late can be seen as an insult.

Guatemala

✘ You know the "okay" hand signal? Don't do that; it's considered obscene here.

✘ That limp handshake your dad teases you about would be perfectly fine in Guatemala.

India

✗ When jogging or exercising, women should always wear long pants.

✗ Never share food with anyone after it has been on your plate.

✗ Oddly, it's considered an insult to thank your host after a nice meal.

✗ Never touch anyone's head, even to pat a little kid.

Indonesia

✗ Avoid touching anything except the ground with your foot.

✗ During meals, avoid talking until everyone is finished eating.

✗ Do not eat while walking in public.

Japan

✗ Always take off your shoes before going into a home; you'll often be given slippers to wear instead.

✗ When using a bathroom, use the special bathroom-only slippers usually available.

✗ Don't blow your nose in public and especially not at a meal table.

✗ Don't leave chopsticks stuck in a bowl of rice; this is only done at funerals.

Russia

✗ Never show the sole of your shoe to anyone, even by accident.

✗ If you're wearing gloves, make sure to remove them before shaking hands.

Taiwan

✗ No winking!

Commonwealth
Nations

In 1867, Canada became the first British colony to be declared a dominion. This gave the colony self-government within the British Empire. The fad caught on, and 33 years later Australia did the same, followed by New Zealand, and then South Africa. These countries kept their ties to Britain and became known as the British Commonwealth. Today, 53 states make up its total. Here are some quick facts about "the Commonwealth," as it is now known.

The Commonwealth country with the...   is...

Largest population	**India**
Smallest population	**Tuvalu**
Largest land area	**Canada**
Smallest land area	**Nauru**
Largest economy	**India**
Suspended membership	**Fiji**
Newest membership	**Mozambique** and **Cameroon**

All countries of the Commonwealth are equal in status . . . but not in sports! Every four years, the Commonwealth Games, a.k.a. "the Friendly Games," are held in a different member country. The first games were held in Hamilton, Ontario in 1930. Australia is the biggest medal-holder so far in the history of the games, followed by England, Canada, and New Zealand.

When You Grow Up

In only a few years, you will have to choose where to go to for your post-secondary education. (Post means "after," and secondary refers to high school, so post-secondary education comes after high school.) What will you study? Law? Science? History? Music? Where will you attend school? Kingston? Ottawa? Halifax? These are some big choices for students. Thankfully, each year *Maclean's* magazine helps them decide by looking at universities across the country and ranking them. Here are the schools the magazine called the best in 2008.

SCHOOL	LOCATION
University of Victoria	Victoria, BC
Simon Fraser University	Burnaby, BC
University of Waterloo	Waterloo, ON
University of Guelph	Guelph, ON
Memorial University	St. John's, NL
University of New Brunswick	Fredericton, NB
Carleton University	Ottawa, ON
York University	Toronto, ON
University of Regina	Regina, SK
University of Windsor	Windsor, ON
Concordia University	Montreal, QC

Social Studies
Game Page

Fill in the missing letters in these words from inside the Social Studies chapter.
Then use the letters you've filled in to spell the secret phrase at the bottom.

1. HUMAN RESOUR_E_

2. _OMOROS

3. _ABLE ISLAND

4. SRI LAN_A

5. ONT_R_O

6. S_BWAY

7. AN_ORRA

8. MAL_A

9. PUBL_C SAF_TY

10. CR_MWELL

S _ _ _ _ _ L
S _ _ _ _ _ _ _
R O _ _ _!

CHAPTER THREE

World & Weather

Erupting volcanoes! Sky-high waterfalls!
Mountains that scrape the clouds!
The boiling hot molten centre of the Earth!
All that, plus . . . how to make sandcastles!
(Hey, it can't *all* be incredibly exciting . . . .)

Start Climbing

We live in a country of varied landscapes — huge mountain ranges, low-lying marshes, and almost everything in between. Each Canadian province and territory has its highs and lows . . . and here's the list of their highest points.

PROVINCE/TERRITORY	HIGHEST POINT
Newfoundland and Labrador	Mount Caubvik (1,652 m)
Nova Scotia	White Hill (532 m)
Prince Edward Island	Queen's County (142 m)
New Brunswick	Mount Carleton (817 m)
Quebec	Mont D'Iberville (1,652 m)
Ontario	Ishpatina Ridge (693 m)
Manitoba	Baldy Mountain (832 m)
Saskatchewan	Cypress Hills (1,392 m)
Alberta	Mount Columbia (3,747 m)
British Columbia	Fairweather Mountain (4,663 m)
Yukon	Mount Logan (5,959 m)
Northwest Territories	Unnamed peak (2,773 m)
Nunavut	Barbeau Peak (2,616 m)

The Next-Greatest Lakes

The Great Lakes hold one-fifth of the Earth's fresh water. It's not surprising, then, that these lakes are on the list of the biggest lakes in Canada. After the War of 1812, however, it was decided that the four Great Lakes that straddle what is now the Canada-U.S. border — Huron, Superior, Erie, and Ontario — would be shared by the two countries. (The fifth, Lake Michigan, is entirely within the Unites States.) So we have instead a list of the next-greatest lakes: the largest freshwater lakes entirely within Canada.

Great Bear Lake/Northwest Territories

Great Slave Lake/Northwest Territories

Lake Winnipeg/Manitoba

Lake Athabasca/Saskatchewan

Reindeer Lake/
Saskatchewan and Manitoba

Smallwood Reservoir/
Newfoundland and Labrador

Nettilling Lake/Nunavut

Lake Winnipegosis/Manitoba

Lake Nipigon/Ontario

Lake Manitoba/Manitoba

Dubawnt/Nunavut

Amadjuak Lake/Nunavut

LONGEST
Place Names

You can probably fit your address easily on an envelope. But imagine if you lived in one of the places listed below. You'd need a pretty danged big envelope! These are some of the longest place names in the world, along with what they mean in their native languages. Good luck pronouncing them!

1. Krungthepmahanakornamornratanakosinmahintarayuttha-yamahadilokphopnopparatrajathaniburiromudomrajaniwesmaha-satharnamornphimarnavatarnsathitsakkattiyavisanukamprasit
Full name of Krung Thep, a city in Thailand (We call this city Bangkok)/163 letters

TRANSLATION: "The great city of angels, the supreme unconquerable land of the great immortal divinity, the royal capital of nine noble gems, the pleasant city with plenty of grand royal palaces and divine paradises for the reincarnated deity, given by Indra and created by the god of crafting."

2. Tetaumatawhakatangihangakoauaotamateaurehaeaturipukapihi-maungahoronukupokaiwhenuaakitanarahu
Maori name for a hill in New Zealand/92 letters

TRANSLATION: "The place where Tamatea, the man with the big knees, who slid, climbed, and swallowed mountains, known as land eater, played his flute to his loved one." ANOTHER TRANSLATION: "The brow of the hill where Tamatea, with the bony knees who slid and climbed mountains, the great traveller, sat and played on the flute to his beloved."

3. Llanfairpwllgwyngyllgogerychwyrndrobwllllantysiliogogogoch
Village in Wales/58 letters

TRANSLATION: "Saint Mary's Church in the hollow of white hazel near a rapid whirlpool and the Church of Saint Tysilio near the red cave."

4. El Pueblo de Nuestra Señora la Reina de los Angeles de Porciuncula
Former name of Los Angeles, Calif./55 letters

TRANSLATION: "The town of our lady the queen of angels of the little portion."

LONGEST
Names at Home

You don't have to go to Bangkok to fill up a "Welcome To . . ." sign. We've got some pretty long place names right here in Canada. Here are some of the longest.

Dysart, Dudley, Harcourt, Guilford, Harburn, Bruton, Havelock, Eyre and Clyde
Letters: 61   Province: Ontario

Cape St. George-Petit Jardin-Grand Jardin-De Grau-Marches Point-Loretto
Letters: 59   Province: Newfoundland and Labrador

L'Annonciation-de-la-Bienheureuse-Vierge-Marie-de-Nazareth
Letters: 50   Province: Quebec

Stanley Bridge, Hope River, Bayview, Cavendish and North Rustico
Letters: 53   Province: Prince Edward Island

L'Immaculée-Conception-de-la-Bienheureuse-Vierge-Marie
Letters: 47   Province: Quebec

Cours d'eau du Cordon des Terres des Sixième et Septième Rangs
Letters: 51   Province: Quebec

Super Climbers

These 12 mountain climbers have joined a very special club. They each have climbed all of the world's highest mountain peaks. Notice that all 14 of these peaks (listed below) are in Asia. All are higher than 8,000 metres (26,250 feet); that's the minimum for what experts call big mountains. These super climbers are listed in the order in which they achieved this amazing feat. Messner completed his mountain-go-round in 1986.

Reinhold Messner/Italy
Jerzy Kukuczka/Poland
Ehardt Loretan/Switzerland
Carlos Carsolio/Mexico
Krzysztof Wielicki/Poland
Juan Oiarzabal/Spain
Sergio Martini/Italy
Park Young Seok/S. Korea
Hang-Gil Um/S. Korea
Alberto Inurrategui/Spain
Han Wang Yong/S. Korea
Ed Viesturs/United States

PEAK	HEIGHT (M)	(FT.)
Everest	8,850	29,035
K2	8,611	28,250
Kanchenjunga	8,586	28,169
Lhotse I	8,516	27,940
Makalu I	8,463	27,766
Cho Oyu	8,201	26,906
Dhaulagiri	8,167	26,795
Manaslu I	8,163	26,781
Nanga Parbat	8,125	26,660
Annapurna I	8,091	26,545
Gasherbrum I	8,068	26,470
Broad Peak	8,047	26,400
Gasherbrum II	8,035	26,360
Shisha Pangma	8,013	26,289

Mountains
& Chains

A group of mountains that is connected is called a mountain range. When mountain ranges are parallel to one another, they're called a mountain chain. Most people use both terms when referring to groups of mountains that are located near one another. These mountain ranges and chains are listed in order of the height of their highest mountain.

MOUNTAIN RANGE/CHAIN	HEIGHT (M)	(FT.)	CONTINENT
Himalayas	8,850	29,035	Asia
Karakoram	8,611	28,250	Asia
Kunlun Shan	7,719	25,326	Asia
Hindu Kush	7,690	25,230	Asia
Andes	6,823	22,385	South America
Elburz	5,670	18,602	Asia
Ellsworth	4,897	16,066	Antarctica
Alps	4,807	15,771	Europe
Virunga	4,507	14,787	Africa
Sierra Nevada	4,418	14,494	North America
Rocky	4,399	14,433	North America
Cascade	4,392	14,410	North America
Transantarctic	4,354	14,284	Antarctica
Sierra Madre Occidental	4,340	14,239	North America
Atlas	4,165	13,665	Africa
Taurus	3,916	12,848	Asia
Drakensberg	3,482	11,425	Africa
Sulaiman	3,443	11,295	Asia
Pyrenees	3,404	11,168	Europe

Smallest Countries
BY SIZE

Sure, the biggest country in the world is easy to find: it's Russia, which takes up 11 percent of all the land in the world. But what about the smallest countries? These are some of the places you can literally circumambulate (Big word alert! It means to walk all the way around). The smallest country is actually completely surrounded by the city of Rome, Italy. In fact, if you add up the land areas of the first 13 countries on this list, you will still not fill Prince Edward Island!

COUNTRY	CAPITAL	AREA (SQ. KM/SQ. MI.)
Vatican	Vatican City	.44/0.2
Monaco	Monaco	1.95/0.7
Nauru	Yaren District	21/8
Tuvalu	Funafuti	26/9
San Marino	San Marino	61/24
Liechtenstein	Vaduz	160/62
Marshall Islands	Majuro	181/70
St. Kitts and Nevis	Basseterra	261/104
Maldives	Male	300/115
Malta	Valletta	316/122
Grenada	St. George's	344/133
St. Vincent and the Grenadines	Kingstown	389/150
Barbados	Bridgetown	430/166
Antigua and Barbuda	St. John's	442/171
Seychelles	Victoria	455/175

Smallest Countries
BY POPULATION

Many of the countries that have the smallest amount of land also have the smallest populations. But not always. Another way of looking at population is to calculate population density, which means how many people live on an average square kilometre of land. That tells you how crowded some of these places really feel! For example, even though Monaco is on both of these "smallest" lists, it has the title of most densely populated country at 16,620 people per square kilometre (43,046 people per square mile). By comparison, the population density of Canada is 3.3 people per square kilometre (9.27/sq. mi.) — that's one of the lowest in the world!

COUNTRY	POPULATION
Vatican	921
Tuvalu	11,636
Nauru	13,048
Palau	21,093
San Marino	29,973
Monaco	32,409
Liechtenstein	33,717
Saint Kitts and Nevis	38,958
Marshall Islands	63,174
Dominica	72,514
Seychelles	82,247
Andorra	82,627
Antigua and Barbuda	84,552
Grenada	90,343

Fun AT THE Poles

The North Pole and the South Pole are considered to be the top and bottom of our planet. At the top, the North Pole is made up of ocean and ice, while on the bottom, the South Pole is made up of land and ice. One is mostly ocean; one is a continent. Here are some fun facts about each.

The North Pole and the Arctic Region

* Pole is located at 90° north latitude.
* Ocean area is 14,090,000 sq. km (5,440,000 sq. mi.).
* A drifting polar ice cap covers the central surface of the Arctic.
* Ice cap is about 3 m (10 ft.) thick.
* Land regions include parts of Asia, Europe, and North America.
* The United States, Canada, Russia, Finland, Sweden, Norway, and Denmark all make claims to parts of the Arctic.
* A submarine first crossed under the North Pole in 1958.
* Some Aboriginal people live in the area, but the Arctic is mostly populated by researchers.

The South Pole and Antarctica

* Pole is located at 90° south latitude.
* Pole is 3,000 m (9,800 ft.) above sea level.
* Land area is 14,000,000 sq. km (5,404,000 sq. mi.).
* Ocean area is also called the Southern or Antarctic Ocean.
* Ice here equals 90 percent of the world's ice.
* Holds 70 percent of the world's fresh water.
* South Pole ice formed about 20 million years ago.
* Roald Amundsen of Norway led first group of explorers to the South Pole on December 14, 1911.
* Between 1,046 and 4,415 people – all researchers and support people – live in Antarctica, depending on the season.

Emissions Report

Canada has one of the worst records for greenhouse gas emissions in the world. Greenhouse gases are a major contributor to global warming. According to information gathered by the Canadian Government, here are the companies responsible for the most greenhouse gas emissions, and their increase (+) or decrease (-) in emissions from the year before (2005–2006).

COMPANY	% INCREASE (+) OR DECREASE (-)
Transalta Corporation	0%
Ontario Power Generation	-18%
Imperial Oil Limited	+6%
Saskatchewan Power Corporation	-2%
CU Inc	0%
Suncor Energy Inc	16%
Epcor Power LP	9%
Emera Incorporated	-8%
Transcanada Corporation	-2%
Shell Canada Ltd	-1%

Types of Maps

A cartographer — a person who makes maps — would able be to make all of these kinds of maps. Some may be in the glove compartment of your family's car, and some are so specialized that you may never have heard of them. There seems to be a type of map to answer any geographical question.

TYPE OF MAPS	WHAT THEY SHOW
Physical	Land and water forms, using colour
Political	Political boundaries, using colour
Relief	Elevation, using shading
Topographic	Elevation of areas, using contour lines

SPECIALTY MAPS	WHAT THEY SHOW
Annual Precipitation	Precipitation in specific areas during the year
Climate	Weather, rainfall, fronts
Economic	Natural and man-made resources
Energy	Distribution and use of types of energy
Ethnic	Distribution of ethnic groups of people
Historical	Land and water features from past views
Languages	Languages spoken in specific areas
Mineral	Location of specific minerals
Natural Hazards	Location of storm paths, volcanoes, earthquakes, etc.
Orthophoto	Land areas, using photographs
Population	Density of people, animals in specific areas
Poverty	Distribution of wealth among people in an area
Railroad	Railroad lines
Road	Highways, roads, distances, points of interest
Time Zone	Earth divided into the 24 time zones
Vegetation	Distribution of vegetation, tropical to desert regions
Water Resources	Available fresh water in the area
Waterways	Location and depth of all waterways

Line 'em Up

Our globes and maps are crisscrossed by lines of latitude and longitude. They help us pinpoint exact locations on the globe, using measurements called degrees (symbol: °). Each degree of latitude and longitude can be divided into 60 minutes (symbol: '), and each minute can be divided into 60 seconds (symbol: "). When using latitude and longitude, the latitude is always listed first.

Lines of Latitude Facts

- Latitude lines measure north and south, from 0° to 90°.
- The lines are an equal distance from one another, about 110 km (69 miles) apart.
- Latitude lines never touch or cross other latitude lines.
- 0° latitude is also called the Equator and is not north or south.
- 23.5° north latitude is called the Tropic of Cancer.
- 23.5° south latitude is called the Tropic of Capricorn.
- The area between the Topic of Cancer and the Tropic of Capricorn is the Tropic Zone.
- 66.5° north latitude is called the Arctic Circle.
- 66.5° south latitude is called the Antarctic Circle.

Lines of Longitude Facts

- Longitude lines, also called meridians, measure east and west from 0° to 180°.
- The lines are vertical and are widest apart at the Equator.
- 0° longitude is also called the Prime Meridian.
- 0° latitude crosses 0° longitude in the Atlantic Ocean off the west coast of Africa.
- 180° longitude is also called the International Date Line.
- The 24 time zones follow longitude lines, changing one hour for every 15°.

Are We Here Yet?

If you were to take the Trans-Canada Highway from St. John's, Newfoundland, to Victoria, B.C., it would take you about a week to drive the whole distance (7,821 km/4,860 miles). That's a long time in a car. So here are some stops you'll want to make along the way to make your trip more fun — Canada's top theme parks!

PARK	LOCATION
Sandspit Cavendish Beach	Hunter River, Prince Edward Island
Upper Clements Park	Annapolis Royal, Nova Scotia
Magic Mountain Water Park	Moncton, New Brunswick
Valcartier Vacation Village	Valcartier, Quebec
La Ronde	Montreal, Quebec
Ontario Place	Toronto, Ontario
Canada's Wonderland	Maple, Ontario
Marineland	Niagara Falls, Ontario
Galaxyland Amusement Park	Edmonton, Alberta
Playland	Vancouver, British Columbia

Are We There Yet?

Millions of tourists come to Canada from the United States, Europe, and Asia each year. Millions more travellers are Canadians exploring other provinces. These are the most popular tourist sites in Canada, and the number of people who visit there each year.

SITE	NUMBER OF VISITORS PER YEAR
Niagara Falls, Niagara Falls	12–14 million
Harbourfront Centre, Toronto	12 million
Granville Island, Vancouver	10–12 million
Stanley Park, Vancouver	8 million
Vieux Port, Montreal	7 million
Exhibition Place, Toronto	4.5–5.2 million
The Forks, Winnipeg	4-5 million
Banff National Park, Alberta	3.3 million
Canada's Wonderland, Maple, Ontario	3.25 million
Le Vieux Québec (Old City), Quebec City	3.02 million
Mont Royal Park, Montreal	3 million

Craters on Earth

Just like the moon, the Earth's surface has been struck by asteroids and comets over the centuries. You can easily see these craters on the moon (the biggest ones form the dark features that we call the Man in the Moon). But on Earth many of the craters are covered by vegetation or are deep under the sea. Some have filled up with water and are now lakes. More than 160 such craters have been documented; here is a list of the 15 biggest. How big is big? The Vredefort crater would stretch from Calgary to Edmonton!

CRATER	DIAMETER (KM/MI.)	LOCATION
Vredefort	300/186.4	South Africa
Sudbury	250/155.3	Canada
Chicxulub	170/105.6	Mexico
Manicouagan	100/62.1	Canada
Popigai	100/62.1	Russia
Acraman	90/55.9	Australia
Chesapeake Bay	90/55.9	United States
Puchezh-Katunki	80/49.7	Russia
Morokweng	70/43.5	South Africa
Kara	65/40.4	Russia
Beaverhead	60/37.3	United States
Tookoonooka	55/34.2	Australia
Charlevoix	54/33.6	Canada
Kara-Kul	52/32.3	Tajikistan
Siljan	52/32.3	Sweden

ACTIVE Volcanoes

They only make the news when they blow their tops, but these volcanoes are always active. They can be found all over our planet. The volcanoes on this list have displayed recent activity, whether that's venting steam or smoke, or actually spewing hot lava.

VOLCANO	LOCATION	VOLCANO	LOCATION
Arenal	Costa Rica	Kilauea	Hawaii
Asama	Japan	Manam	Papua New Guinea
Aso	Japan	Mayon	Philippines
Awu	Indonesia	Mount St. Helens	United States
Bagana	Papua New Guinea	Nyamuragira	Congo
Bezymianny	Russia	Nyiragongo	Congo
Colima	Mexico	Ol Doinyo Lengai	Tanzania
Concepción	Nicaragua	Rabaul	Papua New Guinea
Dukono	Indonesia	Sakura-jima	Japan
Erebus	Antarctica	San Cristobal	Ecuador
Erta Ale	Ethiopia	Sangay	Ecuador
Etna	Italy	Semeru	Indonesia
Fuego	Guatemala	Shishaldin	United States
Glaeras	Colombia	Shiveluch	Russia
Grimsvötn	Iceland	Soputan	Indonesia
Karangetang	Indonesia	Stromboli	Italy
Karymsky	Russia	Tungurahua	Ecuador
Kerinci	Indonesia	Veniaminof	United States

Coral Reefs

Warm, shallow water and sunlight provide a great environment for coral reefs. A coral reef consists of tiny animals that deposit calcium on the sea floor. When the animals die, their exoskeletons (yes, their skeleton is on the outside of their body! Must be fun at Halloween!) pile up to form the basis for the reef. The reef then becomes a home for more living coral, plants, fish, and other marine life.

Types of Reefs

Atoll reef   Continuous barrier reef around a lagoon

Barrier reef   Reef that is separated from the shore by a lagoon

Fringing reef   Reef platforms that extend out from the shoreline

The World's Three Biggest Reefs

1. **Great Barrier Reef**   Queensland, Australia
2. **Barrier Reef of Belize**   Belize, Central America
3. **Indonesian Coral Reefs**   Around Indonesia

Reef Brief

• A temperature of 18°C (65°F) and higher in the winter is needed to support a coral reef, so coral reefs are found in the tropical and subtropical regions of the world's oceans.

• The Great Barrier Reef is the world's largest protected marine area. It is home to more than 4,000 species of mollusks, 1,500 species of fish, 215 bird species, and 16 different types of sea snake.

• If the Great Barrier Reef ran across the Canadian mainland, it would stretch from Vancouver almost all the way to Winnipeg! (Of course, if it did, it wouldn't be as wet.)

HIGHEST Waterfalls

You could take a high dive over these highest waterfalls, but it would be a very long way to the bottom! In comparison to these mighty cataracts (a fancy name for a waterfall), Niagara Falls (on the border between Ontario and New York State) is only 53.6 m (176 ft.) high.

WATERFALL	LOCATION	HEIGHT [M]	(FT.)
Angel	Venezuela	1,000	3,281
Tugela	South Africa	914	3,000
Utigord	Norway	800	2,625
Monge	Norway	774	2,540
Mutarazi	Zimbabwe	762	2,499
Yosemite	United States	739	2,425
Pieman	Australia	715	2,346
Espelands	Norway	703	2,307
Lower Mar Valley	Norway	655	2,151
Tyssestrengene	Norway	647	2,123
Cuquenan	Venezuela	610	2,000
Sentinel	United States	610	2,000
Dudhsagar	India	600	1,969
Sutherland	New Zealand	580	1,904
Kjell	Norway	561	1,841

? How did Angel Falls get its name? American pilot Jimmy Angel flew his airplane near the falls in 1933 while looking for a place to start a mine. He returned later to land atop the mountain from which the falls, well . . . fall. His plane got stuck and it took him 11 days to climb down!

How Dry Are We?

The award for the driest place in the world goes to the Atacama Desert in Chile. That area averages about 0.01 cm (0.004 in.) of rain per year. Some areas of that desert haven't had rain in recorded history. Yet some people do live there. Scientists study the Atacama Desert to find out what kinds of organisms (other than people, who can buy water if they need it) can live in these ultra-dry conditions. Here are the world's driest places.

PLACE	AVERAGE ANNUAL RAINFALL	
	CM	IN.
Atacama, Chile	0.01	0.004
Arica, Chile	0.03	0.012
Al'Kufrah, Libya	0.03	0.012
Aswan, Egypt	0.03	0.012
Luxor, Egypt	0.03	0.012
Ica, Peru	0.09	0.035
Wadi Halfa, Sudan	0.10	0.039
Iquique, Chile	0.20	0.079
Pelican Point, Namibia	0.32	0.126
Aoelef, Algeria	0.48	0.189
Callao, Peru	0.48	0.189

Tropical Rainforests

Tropical rainforests are located within the Earth's tropic zones, which are near the Equator all around the globe. The Tropics of Cancer and Capricorn (see page 89) mark the borders of this area. Only six percent of the world's land is rainforest. The Amazon rainforest in South America is the largest, and also has the widest diversity of plants and animals. Here are some other facts about these important ecosystems.

💧 Tropical rainforests receive anywhere from 150 cm (60 in.) to 1,000 cm (400 in.) of rain each year. Average temperatures range from 20° to 32° C (70° F to 90° F).

💧 Tropical rainforests can be found on the continents of Africa, Asia, and South America.

PERCENT OF THE WORLD'S TROPICAL RAINFORESTS

Africa, Madagascar	19%
Asia, Pacific Islands, Australia	25%
Central and South America	56%

💧 Tropical rainforests can be categorized by their wet and dry seasons.

Flooded forests	rain throughout the year, flooded throughout the year
Seasonally dry forests	dry and wet seasons
Seasonally flooded forests	rain throughout the year with some months of flooding

💧 Tropical rainforests have four layers.

Forest floor	floor of the forest with some plants, receives little direct sunlight
Understory	small trees and plants that grow under the canopy
Canopy	tops of the trees that form a canopy-like cover over the whole forest
Emergent	topmost layer, trees that tower above the rest of the forest

💧 Countries with the most tropical rainforest area.

Brazil	2,915,956 sq. km (1,125,857 sq. mi.)
Indonesia	938,267 sq. km (362,267 sq. mi.)
Dem. Rep. of Congo	604,369 sq. km (233,348 sq. mi.)

Spelunking, Anyone?

Do you want to explore unknown lands, deep and mysterious? Try exploring caves! The sport is called caving, potholing, or spelunking, and the adventurers who love it often find new caves or deeper passages in existing caves. That means this listing of deepest caves can change rapidly. Here's something to think about: A kilometre is 1000 metres (3,281 ft.), so all of these caves descend more than a kilometre below the surface!

CAVE/COUNTRY	DEPTH (M)	(FT.)
Krubera Cave/Abkhazia*	2,191	7,188
Illyuzia-Mexhonnogo/Abkhazia*	1,753	5,751
Lamprechtsofen/Austria	1,632	5,354
Gouffre Mirolda/France	1,626	5,335
Reseau Jean Bernard/France	1,602	5,256
Torca del Cerro del Cueveon/Spain	1,589	5,213
Sarma/Abkhazia*	1,543	5,062
Cehi 2/Slovenia	1,533	5,030
Shakta Vjacheslav Pantjuknina/Abkhazia*	1,508	4,948
Sistema Cheve/Mexico	1,484	4,869

*An autonomous republic within the country of Georgia

Which of these words is *not* used by cavers to describe some sort of cave feature? *Chimney, drapery, gork, grike, hall, meander, passage, pillar, pipe, tunnel.* The answer? All those terms describe features of a cave except *gork.*

AROUND
The World

Many people have made the long trip around the world — some faster than others. The first to circle the globe were aboard the British ship *Victoria*, which took three years to make the trip in 1522. Since then, people have circumnavigated the world (gone all the way around) in just about every sort of vehicle you can think of. Here's a list of some of the most important or record-setting trips. And although the world's been around for quite a while, you can see from this list that people are still finding newer and faster ways to get around it.

TRAVELLERS	TRAVELLED BY	DATES	TIME
Hugo Eckener	Graf Zeppelin airship	1929	21 days
USS Triton	submarine (without surfacing)	1960	61 days
Dave Kunst	foot	1970–1974	1,573 days
Saloo and Neena Choudhury	car	1989	70 days
Kay Cottee	boat (nonstop)	1987–1988	189 days
Steve Fossett	gas balloon	2002	14 days
Chris and Erin Ratay	motorcycles	1999–2003	4 years
Alastair Humphreys	bicycle	2001–2005	1,555 days
Michael and Sandy Groves	SUV	2003–2005	815 days
Steve Fossett	jet (without refuelling)	2005	67 hours
Bruno Peyron and crew	sailboat	2005	51 days

21 Pairs of Shoes

Dave Kunst left his hometown of Waseca, Minnesota, in June 1970. He didn't get back home for more than four years! Where was he? Well, literally, all around the world. It took Dave that long to walk completely around the globe. His mega-power-walk ended up covering 23,255 km (14,450 miles). Along the way, the foot-weary traveller (hasn't he heard of airplanes?!) wore out 21 hard-working pairs of shoes!

PLACES WITH
Food Names

Do you have a hankering for a donut? Cake? A soda? Dig into a map of Canada. Donut Lake is in Manitoba, Cake Bay is in the Northwest Territories and Soda Creek is in British Columbia. Here are some more Canadian places with food names.

Apple River, NS

Bacon Cove, NL

Burgerville, QC

Cape Onion, NL

Carrot River, SK

Cheeseborough, ON

Cherryville, BC

Cinnamon Hills, AB

Cranberry Coulee, SK

Curryville, NB

Driedmeat Creek, AB

Fudge Lake, MB

Ginger Hill, AB

Honey Harbour, ON

Lac au Pécan, QC

Lemonville, ON

Mayo, QC

Meat Cove, NS

Milk Lake, ON

Nut Bay, SK

Olive Lake, SK

Peas Brook, NS

Pickle Lake, ON

Pork and Bean Point, MB

Pork Chop Pit, NL

Raisin Lake, MB

Raspberry, BC

Sugarloaf Mountain, NB

Tomato Creek, AB

Turkey Creek, ON

Walnut, ON

Wienerwurst Mountain, YT

Tasty Places

Over there on page 100 are places named for food; here's a page where we return the favour. A number of well-known foods are named after places. However, sometimes the geographic reference will throw you a curve. For example, Philadelphia cream cheese was invented in Chester, New York. Enjoy a tour of the world with these globe-trotting foods.

PLACE	FOOD
Alaska	**Baked Alaska**
Boston, Mass.	**Boston baked beans**
Boston, Mass.	**Boston cream pie**
Brazil	**Brazil nut**
Brussels, Belgium	**Brussels sprouts**
Canada	**Canada Dry® ginger ale**
Cayenne, French Guyana	**Cayenne pepper**
Cheddar, England	**Cheddar cheese**
Frankfurt am Main, Germany	**Frankfurter**
Hamburg, Germany	**Hamburger**
New York City	**Manhattan clam chowder**
Beijing, China	**Peking duck**
Tabasco, Mexico	**Tabasco sauce**
Worcester, England	**Worcestershire sauce**
Yorkshire, England	**Yorkshire pudding**

Learn to Love Them

Okay, we all know that nobody likes Brussels sprouts. Well, almost nobody. In case you won't eat them, here are some facts to chew on: They are a form of cabbage. They were first described in 1587. And yes, no matter what you think, they are indeed good for you.

See . . . Shells

You know that tongue twister "She sells seashells by the seashore?" Before you (or she) sell any seashells, you have to find them! The shells that we gather come from mollusks and are the exoskeletons of the animals. The two main types of mollusk shells people collect are univalves (the shell is all in one part, like a snail) and bivalves (the shell comes in two parts, like a clam). Here are some popular examples of each type.

Univalves
Abalone
Bubble shells
Common sundials
Conchs
Cone shells
Cowries
Dove shells
Helmet shells
Limpets
Marginellas
Moon shells
Murexes
Nerites
Periwinkles
Slipper shells
Snails
Star shells
Top shells
Tritons
Turban shells
Turrids
Whelks
Wentletraps
Volutes
Worm shells

Bivalves
Ark shells
Bittersweets
Clams
Cockles
False angel wings
Jewel boxes
Jingle shells
Kitten's paws
Lucines
Mussels
Oysters
Pen shells
Scallops
Shipworms

Sandcastle Secrets

Whether you're a king, or a princess, or your name is just Duke, you can own a castle — as long as it's made of sand! Sandcastles can be built in your backyard sandbox or next to the water's edge. From simple mounds to elaborately carved walls and turrets, your castle can be as amazing as your creativity (and patience) allow. Here are some tips from experts on what you need for a simple castle.

The Basics

Sand: Wet sand near the water's edge works best.

Water: Add water as the sand dries out.

Bucket: How else can you carry the sand and water?

Shovel: It's useful for the major digging.

Other tools

Table utensils: Knives, forks, and spoons for smoothing and decorating.

Spray bottle: Filled with water, to keep the sand moist.

Plastic food containers: To mold various shapes for the castle.

Other tools for molding sand: These can include a melon baller, measuring cups, pastry knife, meat mallet, paint scrapers, trowels, putty knives, and paintbrushes.

Tips

▲ Pick a spot away from incoming waves.

▲ Start with a big pile of sand and work from the top down, sculpting as you go.

▲ For stairs, form a ramp first and then cut the stairs in.

▲ A paintbrush is useful for brushing away excess sand.

▲ Spray lightly with water as you finish each section to hold it firm.

▲ Want to go really big? The pros sometimes use wooden forms to create big shapes!

World & Weather
Game Page

This is a book of lists, of course, but sometimes things end up on the wrong list. In this game, read over these mini-lists of words and terms from this chapter. One of the terms doesn't belong; just find the item that's in the wrong list. Then, fill in a few words that briefly describe what the list is about (minus the "wrong" one, of course). For example, which of "rain, snow, sheep, and sleet" doesn't belong? Sheep, right? But that's an easy one. Good luck!

1. **Epcor, Shell, Stremco, Emera, Suncor:** _____

2. **Atlas, Cascade, Barriers, Kush, Alps:** _____

3. **Palau, Monaco, Vatican, Malta, Seychelles:** _____

4. **Niagara, Banff, Granville, Mont Royal, Sealand:** _____

5. **Cherryville, Olive Lake, Turkey Creek, Buttertown, Walnut:** _____

6. **Manam, Mayon, Miami, Asama, Awu, Aso:** _____

7. **Al-Aqsa, Aoelef, Arica, Atacama, Aswan:** _____

8. **Kunst, Fossett, Gordon, Peyron, Cottee:** _____

9. **Ethnic, Monkey, Road, Relief, Mineral:** _____

10. **Whelks, Tritons, Conchs, Volutes, Corks:** _____

Science

Chemistry, botany, dinosaurs — rah!
Stinky plants, yucky skin, passing gas — ha!
C'mon, who says science is boring?
This chapter proves 'em all wrong!

GREAT
Galaxy Names

We are not alone. Astronomers have identified more than 500,000 galaxies in addition to our home galaxy, the Milky Way. The galaxies closest to us, plus any that are studied often, usually get names. Some of those star-studded names are listed below.

Just a lucky few get names, though. Because there are so many galaxies, there just aren't enough names to go around. So all the galaxies also get numbers. For example, the Lost Galaxy (which obviously has been found, or else it wouldn't have a name!) is NGC 4535 (NGC stands for New General Catalogue, an international listing of heavenly bodies).

Andromeda	Hercules A	Seashell
Aquarius Dwarf	Hydra A	Shapley-Ames
Bears Paw	Leo I	Siamese Twins
Black Eye	Mice	Silver Coin
Cartwheel	Pancake	Sombrero
Draco Dwarf	Papillon	Sunflower
The Garland	Pinwheel	Whirlpool
Helix	Pisces Cloud	Wild's Galaxy

Galaxy Guide

There are four basic galaxy shapes:

Barred Spiral	Central bar with an arm at each end
Elliptical	Circular to oval, no arms
Irregular	Clouds of stars, no defined shape
Spiral	Arms of stars curve out from a centre

What's in Here?

If you split the Earth in half (in your imagination, please!), or just cut out a wedge like a piece of cake, you would see the layers of matter that make up the Earth. We spend our lives on the top layer, which is called the crust. Below that are kilometres of other stuff, both squishy and solid. For instance, if you really wanted to dig a hole to China, you'd have to tunnel through hot molten rock. Have fun!

LAYER	WHERE IT IS	WHAT IT IS
Atmosphere	Surrounds the Earth	Air
Crust	Surface of the Earth	Layer of soil and rock
Mantle	Under the crust	Layer of hot, molten rock
Outer core	Centre of the Earth	Layer of hot, molten rock
Inner core	Centre of the Earth	Solid rock

LAYERS OF THE OCEANS

Photic/Topmost layer

Bathyl/Middle layer

Abyssal/Bottom layer

How deep into the Earth have human beings gone? That honour goes to a group of cavers who have explored the deepest cave on Earth. The Krubera Cave in the central Asian nation of Abkhazia has been mapped as far as 2,191 m (7,188 ft.) below the surface. But even that is only a tiny fraction of the distance (6,378 km/3,963 miles) to the centre of the Earth.

Phases of the Moon

The moon is the same size and shape all the time, but from our position on Earth it seems to change shape as it orbits the Earth every 29 days. These apparent changes are called phases, and are caused by the Earth blocking light from the sun so it can't shine on the moon. At different parts of the moon's orbit, different areas of its surface are blocked. It's all an illusion, but we have names for each phase, anyway.

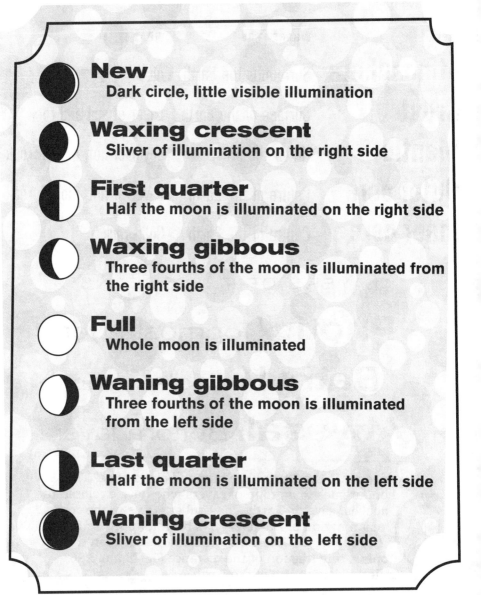

New
Dark circle, little visible illumination

Waxing crescent
Sliver of illumination on the right side

First quarter
Half the moon is illuminated on the right side

Waxing gibbous
Three fourths of the moon is illuminated from the right side

Full
Whole moon is illuminated

Waning gibbous
Three fourths of the moon is illuminated from the left side

Last quarter
Half the moon is illuminated on the left side

Waning crescent
Sliver of illumination on the left side

Who's in the Moon?

Have you ever seen the Man in the Moon? What about Grand MaMoon? Over the years, many people have looked up at the moon and seen, in the dark and light patches of its surface, a man's or woman's face. Look up at a full moon and use your imagination to find the figures listed below. They come from tales told by various cultures around the world. And remember, despite the holes, the moon is not made of cheese.

The Lady in the Moon

○ A Chinese story tells of Chang Er, who drank the elixir of life and flew to the moon.

○ In Mayan mythology, Ix Chel, the Lady Rainbow, is the moon goddess.

○ In Roman mythology, Diana is the goddess of the moon.

○ In Greek mythology, Artemis is the goddess of the moon.

○ In Maori legend, Rona is the woman in the moon, and she carries a bucket of water.

The Man in the Moon

○ A Chinese story tells of Wu Kang, banished to the moon because he was impatient with his life.

○ An Australian Aborigine legend says the man in the moon is a creature named Bunyip, who climbed a tree and stared at everything with one eye. That eye became the moon.

○ In Aztec mythology, Huitzilopochtli cut off Coyolxauhqui's head. He threw it into the sky and it became the moon.

○ In Hindu mythology, the moon god, Soma, travels across the sky in a chariot pulled by white horses.

○ In Japanese legend, Tsuki-Yomi, the moon god, lives on the moon.

The Rabbit in the Moon

○ In this Chinese tale, because the rabbit offered his body as food for the wise sages, he was allowed to live in the Moon Palace and was called the Jade Rabbit.

Space Shuttle
Trips

The space shuttle has provided us with a way to travel back and forth to space from Earth. The official name of the space shuttle program is Space Transportation System, or STS for short, because the main job of the shuttle is to carry stuff — it's like a big space truck. The shuttles have carried payloads (cargo) and astronauts to the International Space Station, launched equipment farther into space, and even taken astronauts to fix the stuff that's already up there. More than 115 space shuttle missions have been launched. Here's a complete list of how many missions each shuttle has flown.

SHUTTLE NAME	FIRST LAUNCHED	NO. OF FLIGHTS
*Columbia**	April 12, 1981	28
*Challenger***	April 4, 1983	10
Discovery	August 30, 1984	32
Atlantis	October 3, 1985	27
Endeavor	May 7, 1992	19

*In 2003, *Columbia* broke up during re-entry, killing all seven of its crew.

**Challenger* exploded during liftoff in 1986; all seven astronauts died.

Shuttle Stuff

The space shuttle provides endless lists of stuff. From the list of animals who have flown in it to the list of food the astronauts eat up there (see page 235), life on the space shuttle is one big checklist. Here's a list of interesting facts about the space shuttle with which to amaze your friends and impress your teachers.

The *Endeavor* space shuttle cost $2.1 billon to build.

The shuttle is 56.08 m (184 ft.) long.

The orbiter has a wingspan of 24 m (78 ft.).

The shuttle weighs 2.04 million kg (4.5 million lb.); that's about equal to 150 school buses!

The maximum payload (how much it can carry) is 26,786 kg (59,000 lb.); that's as much as the weight of two school buses.

Countdown for a shuttle launch actually begins three days before the launch.

Landing delays have been caused by cloud cover, rain, high wind, fog, and low visibility.

In 1995, yellow flicker woodpeckers (yes . . . birds!) pecked 195 holes in the external tank foam of *Discovery*, causing a launch delay.

The shuttle reaches altitudes of between 322 and 620 km (200 and 385 miles) while orbiting the Earth.

The longest mission was *Columbia* in 1996; it lasted 17 days, 53 minutes, 18 seconds.

Junk in Space

Human beings have been shooting stuff into space since the 1950s. A lot of it is still up there! There are now more than 9,000 objects larger than a baseball floating around as "space junk." Even a postage-stamp-size paint chip can cause great damage to a spacecraft, so all that stuff can be dangerous. (The space shuttles have needed more than 80 window replacements because of damage caused by space junk hitting them at top speeds of 35,000 kph/22,000 mph.) Some stuff has fallen toward Earth; most of that burns up on the way in, but some of it plunks down on the ground. Here's a list of some of the things that are still up there, whizzing above our heads.

50 Delta rocket
upper stages
Blown-off hatches
Insulation

Lost glove
Main fuel tank
Metal mesh
Non-working satellites
Paint chips
Pressurization sphere
Trash bags
Nuts and bolts
Skylab chunks
Solar cells
Solid fuel fragments
Space probes
Titanium sphere
Working satellites*

(*We know where all of those are!)

More Than Just  Tang®

Many products we take for granted did not exist before the space program invented them, or developed the materials or the technology used to make them. Scientists had specific needs for space travel and they developed products to answer these needs. These inventions first used in the space program now benefit us in our everyday lives. By the way, Tang was a powdered orange drink later sold to the public as the "stuff that the astronauts drink."

Bar coding

Dust buster

Ear thermometer

Emergency response robot

Enriched baby food

Fire-resistant fabric

Flat-panel TV

Fogless goggles

Freeze-dried food

Hang gliders

Home security system

Joystick controller

Magnetic liquids

Medical imaging

Portable power tools

Satellite TV

Scratch-resistant lenses

Self-righting life raft

Smoke detector

Tap water purifier

Trash compactor

Virtual reality

Voice-controlled wheelchair

Chemistry Basics

Do you like experimenting with liquids that change colours or make a big stink? Congratulations — you like chemistry! Chemistry is the science of how stuff (also known as matter) combines with other stuff. Here is a list of some of the basic terms you'll see in chemistry.

Atom
The smallest part of an element that still has all the properties of the element.

Capillary action
When liquid rises through a small tube or opening.

Chemical reaction
When substances combine and change.

Compound
Two or more elements joined together to form a new substance.

Dispersion
When the particles of a substance scatter throughout another substance.

Dissolve
Adding solids or gases to liquids so that they disappear in the liquid.

Element
A substance made of the same kinds of atoms, which cannot be broken down.

Gas
A substance that does not have a definite shape or volume, but tends to keep expanding.

Liquid
A substance that has definite volume but no definite shape.

Matter
Anything that has volume and mass (size and weight). It comes in three states: solid, liquid, and gas.

Melting point
The temperature at which a solid changes and melts into a liquid.

Molecule
A group of two or more atoms that are joined together.

Neutron
A subatomic particle within the nucleus of the atom; it has no electrical charge.

Periodic table
A list of all the elements, by their atomic number (the number of protons found in the nucleus).

Proton
A subatomic particle within the nucleus of the atom; it has a positive charge.

Sediment
The material that settles at the bottom of a liquid.

Solid
A substance that has a definite size and shape.

Solution
A liquid mixture with atoms of one substance spread evenly in another substance.

Making It Metric

While up here in Canada we long ago made the move to the metric system, those folks down in the U.S. are still using the "old" way to measure things. Still, we have to communicate with them once in a while, so it's good to speak their language, measurement-wise. For converting measurements back and forth across the border, we have just what you need:

Need to change temperature?

From Fahrenheit (F) to Celsius (C):
Subtract 32 from the F temperature, multiply the difference by 5, and divide the answer by 9.

From Celsius to Fahrenheit:
Multiply the C temperature by 9, divide the result by 5, then add 32.

Need to change volume measurements?

- **1 teaspoon = 5 millilitres**
- **1 tablespoon = 15 millilitres**
- **1 fluid ounce = 30 millilitres**
- **1 cup = 237 millilitres**
- **1 pint = 473 millilitres**
- **1 quart = 0.95 litre**
- **1 gallon = 3.8 litres**

Need to change weight measurements?

1 ounce = 28 grams

3.5 ounces = 100 grams

1 pound = 454 grams

2.20 pounds = 1 kilogram

1 ton = 2,000 pounds = 907 kilograms

Need to change length, width, or distance measurements?

0.0001 inch = 1 millimetre

1 inch = 25 millimetres

1 foot = 30.5 centimetres

1 yard = 914 centimetres

1 fathom = 1.829 metres

1 mile = 1.609 kilometres

Need to change area measurements?

1 square inch = 6.5 square centimetres

1 square foot = 929 square centimetres

1 square yard = 0.836 square metres

1 acre = 0.405 hectare

1 square mile = 2.59 square kilometres

Uni-, Bi-, Tri-, and Beyond

Science involves a lot of counting. You'll run across all sorts of prefixes that describe "how many." (A prefix is a syllable that comes before the main part of the word.) For example, poly means "many" in Greek, and we use it in a lot of English words, such as *polygon* (a shape with many sides), *polydactyl* (having more than the normal number of fingers or toes), and *polyglot* (knowing many languages). Some of these prefixes tell you exactly how many. Check out this list of "how many" prefixes, along with what language they originally came from.

PREFIX	MEANING/ ORIGINAL LANGUAGE	PREFIX	MEANING/ ORIGINAL LANGUAGE
Mono	1/Greek	Oct	8/Latin
Uni	1/Latin	Ennea	9/Greek
Bi	2/Latin	Non	9/Latin
Di	2/Greek	De	10/Latin
Duo	2/Latin	Deca	10/Greek
Tri	3/Latin	Hendeca	11/Greek
Quad	4/Latin	Unde	11/Latin
Quart	4/Latin	Duodec	12/Latin
Tetra	4/Greek	Dodeca	12/Greek
Penta	5/Greek	Centi	100/Latin
Quint	5/Latin	Hecto	100/Greek
Hexa	6/Greek	Milli	1,000/Latin
Sex	6/Latin	Kilo	1,000/Greek
Sept	7/Latin	Mega	1 million/Greek
Hepta	7/Greek	Giga	1 billion/Latin
		Tera	1 trillion/Greek

Power Up!

Need to find the square, cube, or higher power of a number? You can do the multiplication yourself (a lot of work) or use this handy chart (no work at all!) to find your answer.

NUMBER	POWER 2ND	3RD	4TH	5TH	6TH	7TH
2	4	8	16	32	64	128
3	9	27	81	243	729	2,187
4	16	64	256	1,024	4,096	16,384
5	25	125	625	3,125	15,625	78,125
6	36	216	1,296	7,776	46,656	279,936
7	49	343	2,401	16,807	117,649	823,543
8	64	512	4,096	32,768	262,144	2,097,152
9	81	729	6,561	59,049	531,441	4,782,969
10	100	1,000	10,000	100,000	1,000,000	10,000,000
11	121	1,331	14,641	161,051	1,771,561	19,487,171
12	144	1,728	20,736	248,832	2,985,984	35,831,808

Plant Medicine

Many common plants found in homes and gardens can be used for healing. Their uses come down through folklore and experience. Some of these plants are eaten; others are put on the skin. Be careful what you try and eat! These medicines should only be made by someone who knows what they are doing. This list of plants shows the conditions they treat.

Aloe	wounds, burns, sunburn
Anise	coughs
Apples	constipation, high cholesterol
Cabbage	poor digestion, achy joints, skin problems, fever
Cinnamon	colds, arthritis, rheumatism
Eucalyptus	infected wounds, bacterial infections
Garlic	high cholesterol, weak immune system
Ginger	upset stomach, travel sickness, nausea
Ginseng	low energy
Green tea	low energy, digestive problems
Honeysuckle	asthma
Lavender	sleep problems
Licorice	upset stomach
Oats	high cholesterol
Peony	nervous conditions
Peppermint	indigestion
Plantain	constipation
Primrose	headaches, colds
Rhubarb	constipation
Skullcap	nervous disorders, headaches

Tallest Trees

They come in all sorts of sizes but (mostly) in one shape: straight up and down. Trees provide us with air to breathe, fruit to eat, and wood to sit on and live in. Some trees can be real skyscrapers. Here's a list of amazing facts about the world's tallest trees.

Tallest Trees Ever

Loggers in Australia cut down a eucalyptus tree that was 132.6 m (435 ft.) in 1872. A coast redwood that measured 113.4 m (372 ft.) fell in 1991 in California.

Tallest Living Tree

The Stratosphere Giant, also a coast redwood, stands proudly in a secret location (to keep it from being swamped by tourists) in Humboldt Redwoods Park in northern California. It towers 112.7 m (370 ft.). However, in September 2006, scientists found three nearby trees that topped it; if confirmed, the new tallest tree would be a 115.2-m (378-ft.) redwood known as Hyperion.

Tallest Species

Coast redwoods, Australian eucalyptus, Australian flowering mountain ash all can top 100 m (330 ft.).

How Tall Can They Go?

An article in the British journal *Science* reported that the tallest a tree could be is 130 m (426 ft.). Why a limit? Because the taller a tree is, the harder it is for it to get water and food all the way to the top. Rain helps, but trees live mostly on what's inside them, and that's a long elevator ride to the top branches!

MEDICAL
Machines

From machines that measure your heartbeat to robots that perform surgery, no hospital or doctor's office is complete without dozens of machines. Here's a list of some of the more common ones and what they do.

CAT No, not a feline, but a machine that produces a kind of internal picture of a person's body. It stands for Computed Axial Tomography, and delivers an almost 3-D vision of what's going on inside you.

Defibrillator This is the one they use when they yell "Clear!" Two paddles are placed on a person whose heart has stopped. Using electric current from this machine, doctors try to restart the heart.

Dialysis machine When a person's kidneys aren't working, this machine cleans his or her blood. Dialysis machines are like washing machines for blood.

EEG This electroencephalogram measures brain waves.

EKG (or ECG) Using wires attached to a person, the electrocardiogram measures all sorts of information about how the heart is beating. It spits out a graph on a narrow paper strip that a doctor can read.

Pulse oximeter Hooked up to a patient's finger or ear, this machine measures how much oxygen is in the blood.

Ultrasound Another way that doctors look inside us is with this machine. Sound waves bounce in and out and the machine produces a black-and-white still or moving picture.

Types of Doctors

Many doctors practice a special branch of medicine. Depending on your needs and symptoms, you may visit one or more of these specialists someday.

Allergist	immune system, allergies
General Practitioner	general, overall health
Anesthesiologist	uses anesthesia to relieve pain
Cardiologist	circulatory system, heart
Dermatologist	skin
Emergency Physician	emergency treatment
Gastroenterologist	digestive system
Gynecologist	female reproductive system
Hematologist	circulatory system, blood
Neurologist	nervous system
Pathologist	body tissues, secretions, fluids
Pediatrician	babies, kids
Psychiatrist	mental and emotional disorders
Obstetrician	pregnancy
Ophthalmologist	eyes, vision
Oncologist	cancer
Podiatrist	feet
Radiologist	X-rays
Urologist	urinary system

Skin Deep

What's the largest organ of your body? Would you guess the stomach or intestines? Not even close! It's your skin. If you stretched it all out, the skin on an adult covers an area about the size of a shower curtain. Your great big skin is actually made up of three layers. The top layer, the epidermis, is the part you see. It actually renews itself about every 40 days. Below that are other layers that each have a job to do. Here's what's in your skin, from the outside, in.

Epidermis (5 layers)
Stratum corneum
Stratum licidum
Granular layer
Spiny layer
Basal layer

Dermis (2 layers)
Papillary
Reticular

The dermis contains: blood vessels, hair roots, nerves, sweat glands, lymph vessels

Subcutaneous fat (1 layer)

The subcutaneous fat layer contains: adipose fat cells, larger blood vessels, nerves

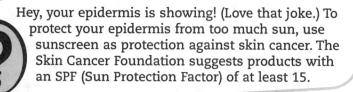

Hey, your epidermis is showing! (Love that joke.) To protect your epidermis from too much sun, use sunscreen as protection against skin cancer. The Skin Cancer Foundation suggests products with an SPF (Sun Protection Factor) of at least 15.

Open Wide!
Types of Teeth

Your first set of teeth, known as the baby or milk teeth, number 20, but the magic number is 32. When all of your adult teeth finally push through your gums, you will have 32 teeth. Human teeth come in these specific categories.

Each jaw has:

4 incisors   x 2 jaws = **8** incisors

2 canine or eye teeth or cuspids   x 2 jaws = **4** canine teeth

4 premolars or bicuspids   x 2 jaws = **8** premolars

6 molars   x 2 jaws = **12** molars

(Your wisdom teeth are the end molars on each side of your upper and lower jaws. You might have four of these, but they may not come in for years — if at all.)

Don't Go to the Dentist — *Be* the Dentist!

Lots of kids grow up wanting to be doctors. But maybe some of you should think about being dentists, too. There are about 18,000 working dentists in Canada, but enrollment at dental schools is only going up a tiny bit each year, and since everyone has teeth, it's a pretty steady job. Plus, after only five years, most dentists make more than $100,000 a year. There's gold in them thar teeth (both for you and the patient!).

Big Body Parts

Think you've got big feet? Take a look at these folks! At the moment these people claim the titles for big body parts, according to Guinness World Records®.

Tallest

Man	Robert Pershing Wadlow, USA	2.72 m/8 ft. 11.1 in.
Woman	Zeng Jinlian, China	2.48 m/8 ft. 1.75 in.
Living man	Xi Shun, China	2.35 m/7 ft. 8.95 in.
Living woman	Sandy Allen, USA	2.31 m/7 ft. 7.25 in.
NBA player	Gheorghe Muresan, Romania	2.31 m/7 ft. 7 in.

Largest/Longest

Arm hair	David Hruska, USA	9.7 cm/3.18 in.
Ear hair	Radhakant Bajpai, India	13.2 cm/5.19 in.
Fingernails	Lee Redmond, USA	7.51 m/295.8 in.
Hair	Xie Qiuping, China	5.63 m/221.54 in.
Hands	Robert Pershing Wadlow, USA	32.3 cm/12.75 in.
Kidney stone	Peter Baulman, Australia	356 g/12.5 oz.
Leg hair	Tim Stinton, Australia	12.4 cm/4.88 in.
Neck	Padaung Tribal Women, Myanmar	40 cm/15.75 in.
Nose (living man)	Mehmet Ozyurek, Turkey	8.8 cm/3.46 in.
Tongue	Stephen Taylor, Britain	9.4 cm/3.7 in.

Heaviest

Twins	Billy Leon McCrary, USA	337 kg/743 lb.
	Benny Lloyd McCrary, USA	328 kg/723 lb.
Sumo wrestler	Chad Rowan (Akebono), USA*	349 kg/501 lb.
Man	Jon Brower Minnoch, USA	635 kg/1,400 lb.
Woman	Rosalie Bradford, USA	544 kg/1,200 lb.

*He's now a Japanese citizen.

Thanks, Sun!

Energy from the sun powers everything on Earth. What's that, you say? Gas powers cars? Well, what do you think helped grow the plants that fed the dinosaurs, who would become oil and gas millions of years later? Solar power is becoming more and more a regular part of people's energy supply. Here are some facts about solar power to impress your friends with. Please wear sunscreen and don't look at the facts directly.

✴ In just one hour, the Earth is hit with more solar power than it uses in a year!

✴ Japan produces half of the world's solar "cells," the devices that gather in the sun's rays and help convert it to electricity.

✴ The OptiSolar Farms Canada project will be the largest solar energy farm in North America. When fully built in Sarnia, the 365-hectare farm will provide enough energy for 20,000 homes.

✴ In some cases, your house's solar cells could produce more electricity than you need. You could then "cell" (ha-ha, get it?) the extra electricity back to the power company; your house could make money!

✴ One of the most popular ways to use solar energy is to heat water. Pipes inside the solar cells heat the water, which is then distributed to the house.

✴ Solar-powered cars? Well, not in your garage yet, but maybe someday. College students and scientists take part in annual competitions to create and race solar-powered cars.

Passing Gas

Gas — the kind cars run on — is expensive, and the world's supply of oil is shrinking. That's why in the future cars may run on plain old vegetable oil. Here is a list of some oil alternatives that are being tested or are already being used to power car engines and other machines. Pass the deep fryer, please!

POWER	WHERE IT COMES FROM
Electricity	Batteries, solar and wind sources
Vegetable oil	Corn and other plant oils; used cooking oil
Hydrogen	Natural gas
Methanol	Alcohol
Ethanol	Distilled corn, barley, wheat
Bioethanol	Trees, grasses
Biodiesel	Blend of vegetable oil and diesel fuel
Propane	By-product of natural gas and oil refining

Hybrids to the Rescue!

If you're concerned about our overuse of oil and gas to power cars, consider a hybrid. They combine an electric motor with a gas engine to greatly reduce gasoline use. Here's a list of the most popular hybrids sold in Canada:

Toyota Prius • Honda Civic • Toyota Camry • Ford Escape • Toyota Highlander • Saturn Vue • Green Line • Honda Accord • Lexus RX400h • Nissan Altima • Honda Insight

Deadliest Dinos

The movies have shown us some deadly dinosaurs, such as the *Tyrannosaurus rex* and *Velociraptor*, and how these meat-eating animals had to hunt, stalk, and chase their food. Their skeletons tell us that they were perfectly designed for these tasks. Sharp teeth and deadly claws made these dinosaurs among the deadliest (to other dinosaurs, anyway).

NAME	WHAT NAME MEANS	LENGTH (M/FT.)
Allosaurus	Different reptile	12.2/40
Daspletosaurus	Frightful lizard	9.1/30
Deinonychus	Terrible claw	4.6/15
Dilophosaurus	Double-crested lizard	7/23
Eotyrannus	Dawn tyrant	4.9/16
Genusaurus	Knee lizard	4/13
Giganotosaurus	Giant southern lizard	12.5/42
Gorgosaurus	Fierce lizard	9/29.5
Megaraptor	Big plunderer	8/26
Neovenator	New hunter	7.0/25
Ornitholestes	Bird robber	2.1/7
Saurophaganax	Reptile-eating master	12.2/40
Tyrannosaurus	Tyrant reptile king	15.2/50
Utahraptor	Utah plunderer	5.9/19.5
Velociraptor	Swift robber	2/6.5

Mellowest Dinos

We assume these plant-eating dinosaurs spent long hours locating food and just grazing. Of course, no humans were around to check! Some of these plant-eaters were pretty fierce-looking, with horns and plates, but they just used them for defense. Here are some dinos that you could have kept as pets (if your backyard were as big as Newfoundland).

NAME	WHAT IT MEANS	LENGTH (M/FT.)
Antarctosaurus	Southern lizard	30.5/100
Apatosaurus	Deceptive reptile	27.4/90
Barosaurus	Heavy lizard	27.1/89
Brachiosaurus	Arm reptile	29.9/98
Diplodocus	Double beam	26.8/88
Hadrosaurus	Bulky lizard	7.6/25
Iguanodon	Iguana tooth	10.1/33
Lurdusaurus	Heavy lizard	9/29.5
Melanorosaurus	Black mountain lizard	12.2/40
Paralititan	Tidal giant	21.3/70
Sauroposeidon	Earthquake god lizard	29.9/98
Seismosaurus	Earthquake lizard	41.1/135
Supersaurus	Super lizard	33.5/110
Triceratops	Three-horned face	9/30
Vulcanodon	Vulcan's tooth	6.5/21

Rarest Plants
in the World

Many of these plants have become rare because their environments have changed or humans have destroyed them. It is estimated that one in eight species could become extinct. A few just don't reproduce fast enough to maintain great numbers, and some have just been discovered. Perhaps the rarest is *Encephalartos woodii*, also called wood cycad. It no longer exists in nature, and only the male species can be found in botanical gardens. A female species of this plant has never been found.

PLANT	LOCATION
Asian slipper orchid	Southwest Asia
Baker's larkspur	California
Daisy tree	Galapagos Islands
Desert yellowhead	Wyoming
Golden larch	Yangtze River Valley, China
Iris sofarana	Lebanon
Jellyfish tree	Seychelles
Lakeside daisy	Ohio
Metasequoia	China
Parachute penstemon	Colorado
Pink tickseed	Nova Scotia
Rosy periwinkle	Madagascar
Short's goldenrod	Indiana
Showy stickweed	Washington
Snowdonia hawkweed	Wales
Wollemi pines	Australia
Yukon-Whitlow grass	Yukon Territory

Stinky Plants

Most flowers smell pretty nice. In fact, people grow some of them, such as lilacs, just for their lovely scent. Then there are the plants listed here — the stinkiest, most awful-smelling plants in the world. The king of the stinky plants is the *Titan arum*, known as the corpse plant. Its odour is described as being like a rotting, dead human body, but when it blooms people rush to smell it — just to say they did! (We don't!) Enjoy these odours — if you dare!

Bear's foot hellebore
Corpse plant
Dragon lily
Durian fruit
Garlic
Ginkgo tree seeds
Hairy giant starfish flower
Onion
Ramps
Sauromatum
Skunk cabbage
Smelly socks grevillea
Smelly wallflower
Stinky rabbitbrush
Voodoo lily

Ditto!

Imagine coming face-to-face with your clone! Do you want someone to create another you, exactly like you? Sounds like science fiction, but for some animals it has become science fact. Scientists take DNA from one animal and "grow" an exact copy. Here are some of the animals that have been successfully cloned.

ANIMAL	NAME	LOCATION	YEAR
Sheep	Dolly	Scotland	1996
Mouse	Cumulina	USA	1997
Cow	2 unnamed calves	Japan	1998
Cow	George, Charlie	USA	1998
Rhesus monkey	Tetra	USA	1999
Wild sheep	Lamb	Italy	2000
Pig	Millie, Christa, Alexis, Carrel, Dotcom	USA	2000
Cat	Copycat	USA	2001
Pig	Noel, Angel, Star, Joy, Mary	Scotland	2001
Mule	Idaho Gem	USA	2003
Horse	Prometea	Italy	2003
Rat	Ralph	France	2003
Dog	Snuppy	S. Korea	2005
Horse	Pieraz Cryozootech Stallion	Italy	2005

A Really Tiny LIST

As tiny as the atom is, there are even smaller subatomic (smaller than an atom) particles. More than 300 subatomic particles have been identified. This list includes a few of those subatomic particles, from the biggest to the really, really, really, really, really, really smallest.

Atoms
   Nucleus
      Elementary Particles
         Quarks
            Up
            Down
            Strange
            Charmed
            Truth (top)
            Beauty (bottom)
         Leptons
            Electron
            Electron Neutrino
            Muon
            Muon Neutrino
            Tau
            Tau Neutrino
         Gauge Bosons
            Photon
            Graviton
            Gluon
            Weakon
      Composite Particles (Hadrons)
         Mesons
            Pion
            Kaon
            Psi
            Upsilon
         Baryons
            Nucleon
            Proton
            Neutron
            Hyperon
            Lambda
            Xi
            Omega

Science
Game Page

Science is about connections, putting things together, and understanding how they interact and work together. In this game, you have to find connections between various things. Look at the three columns of words and create nine triple connections, using one term from each column. The words are usually from related parts of one area of science. The first one is done for you to show you how it works.

Andromeda	Math	Sheep
Ethanol	Tomography	Gas
Dinosaur	Astronomy	Canine
Stratum corneum	Chemistry	Specimen
Incisors	Botanic	Power
Element	Paleontology	Corn
Cloning	Power	Galaxy
Eucalyptus	DNA	Doctor
Deca	Dermatology	Antarctosaurus
CAT	Dentistry	Dermis

CHAPTER FIVE

Words

In this chapter, read about a lot of good stuff, such as what to call *Bang!* and *Zip*, how to find the bathroom in China (and what to call it in ancient Israel), when you can write *Q* without a *U*, and how to Google. See? Good stuff.

THANKS TO THE
Greeks

The ancient Greeks gave our culture many things: democracy, drama, poetry, olive oil. They also left behind thousands of words that have been adopted into English. As you read this list, consider that you are actually reading Greek!

Alphabet*

Athlete

Cemetery

Diploma

Echo

Gymnasium

Hero

Mechanical

Museum

Mystery

Ocean

Olympics

Pylon

Rhythm

Stethoscope

Theatre

Tragedy

*Alpha and beta are the first two Greek letters.

Here is what some planets would be named if Greek gods' names were used instead of Roman: Zeus (Jupiter), Cronos (Saturn), and Poseidon (Neptune). Remember the "old" planet Pluto? The Greek version would be Hades.

THANKS TO THE
Romans

Not long after the Greeks, the Romans came around and conquered much of the known world. They spread their language, Latin, throughout their empire. English takes many, many words and parts of words from Latin. The names of six planets — Mercury, Mars, Venus, Jupiter, Saturn, and Neptune — come from Roman gods. The signs of the zodiac are based on Latin terms. While many English words are based on Latin roots, some Latin words or terms remain unchanged in English. Here are a few well-known ones:

WORD/PHRASE	MEANING
Ad nauseam	Lasting way, way too long
Agenda	List of things to do, a schedule
Alumni	People who graduated from a particular school
Ante meridiem (a.m.)	Before noon
Circa (c.)	About
Circus	Entertainment
i.e. (id est)	"That is"
Percent	Part of 100
Posse	Volunteer group that chases criminals
Post meridiem (p.m.)	After noon
Postscript (P.S.)	A note after the main letter
Pro bono	For free
Subpoena	Legal term for a document calling a person to court
Versus (vs.)	Head-to-head, against
Vice versa	Back and forth, the same one way as another

Building the
Alphabet

The present-day English alphabet has 26 letters, but where did they come from? Turns out that our English alphabet has many sources, but may have first originated from Semitic workers in Egypt, who created their own written shorthand. They passed it on to the Phoenicians, who in turn passed it on to the Greeks, who forwarded it to the Etruscans, who had it snatched away from them by the Romans. Whew! Most letters originally represented objects, but as different cultures adopted the symbols, the letters were turned, reversed, and changed. The Roman or Latin alphabet is closest to what we now use.

SOURCE/POSSIBLE ORIGINAL MEANING

A Greek, Roman/ox

B Greek, Roman/house

C Greek/camel

D Greek, Roman/door

E Greek, Roman/man

F Roman/hook

G Greek, Etruscan, Roman/camel

H Greek, Roman/fence

I Greek, Roman/hand

J   Roman/alternate form for *I*

K   Greek, Roman/palm of the hand

L   Greek, Roman/ox stick

M   Greek, Roman/water

N   Greek, Roman/snake

O   Greek, Roman/eye

P   Greek, Roman/mouth

Q   Etruscan, Roman/monkey

R   Roman/head

S   Greek, Roman/tooth

T   Greek, Roman/mark

U   Roman/alternate form for *V*

V   Etruscan/hook

W   English/double *u*'s

X   Greek, Etruscan, Roman/fish

Y   Greek/hook

Z   Greek, Roman/weapon

SPEAKING "English"

The playwright George Bernard Shaw once said, "England and America are two countries divided by a common language." While Canada is not as different as America, we still have different ways of speaking English than our English cousins. The main difference these days is in slang. Here's a list of words that people in England use every day.

THEIR WAY	OUR WAY
Answerphone	Answering machine
Barrister	Lawyer
Bloke	Man
Bobby	Policeman
Brolly	Umbrella
Bum bag	Fanny pack
Chuffed	Proud or pleased
Crisps	Potato chips
Daft	Odd or kooky
Fairy cake	Cupcake
Fortnight	A period of two weeks
Gobsmacked	Amazed
Grotty	Gross
Knickers	Underwear
Knackered	Tired
Moggy	Alley cat
Oi!	Hey!
Petrol	Gasoline
Pushchair	Baby stroller
Queue	Line of waiting people
Sleeping policeman	Speed bump

Busiest Words

These English words occur most often in general use. The word *word* is the 45th most-used word (there, we just used it twice . . . wait, three times!). The word *list* is 310th on the, um, list.

the	it	are
of	you	with
to	that	as
and	he	I
a	was	his
in	for	they
is	on	

Top 10 Most-Used Verbs

is	be	were
was	have	use
are	had	said
	can	

Looking for the Loo

It's the bathroom. Or the washroom. Or the boys' room/girls' room. You and your family probably have your own names for it, too. You're not alone. Here is a list of other words used — yesterday or today — for this most useful of rooms.

Can
(North American)

Head
(on board ships)

Jakes
(British)

John
(various)

Loo
(British)

House of Honour
(ancient Israel)

**House of
the Morning**
(ancient Egypt)

Necessarium
(ancient Rome)

Privy
(British)

Pot
(North American)

Powder room
(North American)

Restroom
(North American)

Room 100
(popular in Europe)

Seat of ease
(medieval)

W.C.
(abbreviation for *water closet*)

ROOM 100

Really Gotta Go!

There's nothing worse than needing a bathroom — quick! — and not knowing how to ask. To help you avoid this potentially embarrassing problem, here's a list that tells you how to ask "Where is the bathroom?" in a variety of languages. Or you could just look for the signs.

LANGUAGE	"WHERE IS THE BATHROOM?"
Arabic	Ain Alhamaam?
Mandarin	Ce suo zai nali?
Creole	Ki kote twalét-la?
Dutch	Waar is het toilet?
French	Où sont les toilettes?
German	Wo ist die Toilette?
Hawaiian	Aia i hea ka lua?
Italian	Dov'é il bagno?
Japanese	Toire wa doko desu ka?
Latin	Ubi sunt loca secreta?
Polish	Gdzie jest toaleta?
Spanish	¿Donde está el baño?
Swahili	Choo kiko wapi?
Xhosa	Liphi igumbi langasese?
Yiddish	Vu iz dos bodtsimer?

Mark It Up!

Do you ever get a paper back from your teacher and find that it's covered with the footprints of a wandering chicken? Well, we get our work back from our editor like that sometimes. Those scratches and marks and squiggles are really a secret code to improve your (and our) writing. On this list are some of the most common proofreaders' marks. The text on the bottom right shows how they all look on the page.

MARK　　**MEANING**

MARK	MEANING
℘	**Delete, which means remove**
℘	**Delete and close up** (don't leave an empty space!)
#	**Insert a space**
∾	**Switch places** (the fancy word is *transpose*)
¶	**Begin new paragraph**
ⓢⓟ	**Spell out this abbreviation**
☰	**Make a capital letter**
/	**Make a lower-case letter**

Insert a hyphen

Insert a dash (longer than a hyphen)

Insert a comma

Insert an apostrophe

Insert a period

Add quotation marks

Marks in Action!

¶The snarling beast must have weighed 900 lbs. and sported twenty-seven sharp teeth. I shivered in fear as it advanced toward me. "Hey, monster," I said. "How do you cut the ocean?" The riddle stopped it in its tracks. a confused look came over its face. The beast's teeth chattered — a frightening sound as it pondered answer. the "A sea saw!" I yelled. "Get it?" And then I sprinted for the mouth of the cave.

Old as the Hills

Have you ever heard of a simile [*SIM-ah-lee*]? It's a way of describing something by comparing it to something else, using the words *like* or *as*. That pizza was cold as ice. That elephant was as big as a house. Fred swam like a fish. Got it? Some of these comparisons are used way, way too often. When you see these, you know the writer got bored and couldn't think of a new way to say something. Try to avoid using these in your writing. If you do, you'll be as good as gold. (Oops, there's another one!)

Black as night
Busy as a bee
Cold as ice
Difficult as finding a needle in a haystack
Flies like a bird
Gentle as a lamb
Green as the grass
Hard as ice
Jumps like a kangaroo
Old as the hills
Neat as a pin
Nutty as a fruitcake

Pretty as a picture

Proud as a peacock

Quiet as a mouse

Runs like the wind

Shakes like a leaf

Sick as a dog

Sly as a fox

Smells like a skunk

Skinny as a rail

Slow as molasses

Spins like a top

Strong as an ox

Stubborn as a mule

Swims like a fish

Tall as a tree

Tough as nails

White as snow

Talking Sports

You might not know it, but you talk sports all the time. There are dozens and dozens of words, phrases, and expressions in English that come right from the wide world of sports. See if you can think of others from each of these sports. It's a whole new ball game, so we'll give you a sporting chance. If you can't think of any, though, well, that's just the way the ball bounces.

Baseball

Ballpark figure	Rough estimate
Out of left field	From out of nowhere, unexpected
Right off the bat	Right away, immediately
Strike out	Fail
Throw a curve	Fool or surprise or bring up something unexpected

Basketball

The ball's in your court	It's your turn
Slam dunk	Easy to do

Boxing

Against the ropes	About to fail at something, running out of time
Throw in the towel	Give up or quit

Football

Huddle   Gather together

Make an end run   Get around an obstacle
or person, often sneakily

Golf

You aced it!   You got it just right (from *ace*, a term
for a hole in one)

Hockey

Faceoff   A confrontation

Power play   an attempt to gain power in
relationships, politics, or business

Horse racing

Down to the wire   At the last minute, just in time

Kiss It Good-bye!

Baseball announcers often have their own special "home run call." Here's a short list of some famous ones:

"It might be, it could be . . . it is! A home run!" Harry Caray

"Touch 'em all!" Tom Cheek

"Open the window, Aunt Minnie! Here it comes!" Rosey Roswell

"Back, back, back, back . . . gone!" Chris Berman

"Going, going, gone! How about that?!" Mel Allen

Bang! Zip! Ding!

This was one of our favourite lists to write. You should have seen us tossing these words around the room: *Zing! Zap! Zoom!* What kind of words were we throwing? The term for words used to represent a sound is *onomatopoeia*. The idea of these words is to make you see in letters what you might hear with your ears. (By the way, comic books are a great place to see onomatopoeia in action.)

Bam!	Doink!	Tick-tock!
Bang!	Dong!	Splat!
Blam!	Fizz!	Wham!
Beep-beep!	Hiss!	Whap!
Boing!	Kaboom!	Whirr!
Clang!	Ka-ching!	Zip!
Clank!	Plop!	Zap!
Clunk!	Pop!	Zoom!
Ding!	Pow!	

Useful Japanese Phrases

You might not know any Japanese — except maybe *sayonara* (good-bye) and Toyota, but here are some useful words and phrases to know if you ever find yourself in Tokyo. Of course, they are usually written in Japanese characters, so don't expect to see them written this way on a sushi menu in Japan.

ENGLISH	JAPANESE
Do you have this?	**Kore arimasu ka?** (pointing to the picture on the menu)
Excuse me.	**Sumimasen ga.**
Good morning.	**O-hayou gozai masu.**
Is there anyone there who can speak English?	**Sumimasen, eigo ga hanaseru kata irasshaimasu ka?**
My name is _____.	**Watashi no namae wa _____ desu.**
Please take me to a doctor.	**Oisha san ni tsurete itte kudasai.**
I'm sorry.	**Sumi masen.**
Thank you.	**Domo arigatou.**

We've used English letters here, but real Japanese uses characters. There are three sets: 46 *hiranga* that make up most of the basic "alphabet" of the language. There are thousands of *kanji* that represent sounds. Finally, *katakana* are used to write words from other languages in Japanese.

USEFUL
Chinese Phrases

Chinese is a language written with characters rather than an alphabet. That means each word is represented by one character. But there is an official way to spell out the sounds of the Chinese characters; it's called Pinyin. So here are some useful Mandarin Chinese phrases, written in Pinyin. Because you never know — there might come a day when you need to introduce yourself in Chinese.

ENGLISH	CHINESE
Hello.	Ni hao.
My first name is ____, and my last name is ____.	Wo jiao ____ , xing ____.
I am a student.	Wo shi xuesheng.
I am Canadian.	Wo shi Jianadaren.
Do you speak English?	Hui shuo Yingwen ma?
I like to eat Chinese food.	Wo xihuan chi Zong can.
How do you say ____ in Chinese?	____de Zhongwen zenme shuo?
Thank you.	Xie xie.
Good-bye.	Zai jian.

MOTHER Tongue

Canada has two official languages: English and French. But as a multicultural society, we hear the sounds of hundreds of different tongues on our streets every day. According to the Canadian government, a person's "mother tongue" is the language they learned at home when they were children, and which they still understand today. Is yours on this list?

LANGUAGE	APPROXIMATE NUMBER OF SPEAKERS
English	18,056,000
French	6,892,000
Chinese	1,034,000
Italian	476,905
German	466,655
Punjabi	382,585
Spanish	362,120
Arabic	286,785
Tagalog	266,440
Portuguese	229,280
Polish	217,605
Urdu	156,415

¿Cómo Está Usted?

Sunny Mexico, Spain, or any one of several Central and South American countries, are popular vacation spots. These words and phrases might come in handy not only if you travel to a Spanish-speaking country, but if you visit many large cities in the United States. *¡Que bueno!*

ENGLISH	SPANISH
Do you speak English?	¿Habla inglés?
Goodbye.	Adios.
Hello.	Hola.
How are you?	¿Cómo está?
How old are you?	¿Cuantos años tiene?
How's it going?	¿Qué tal?
I am fine, thank you.	Estoy muy bien, gracias.
My name is _____.	Me llamo _____.
Thank you very much.	Muchas gracias.
What time is it?	¿Qué hora es?
Where is the _____?	¿Dónde está el/la_____?
You're welcome.	De nada.

Bonjour!

That's pronounced "bohn-ZHOOR!" and it's French for "Hello!" (It actually means "good day," but it's used like our "hello.") French is a very popular language around the world and is one of Canada's two official languages. Here is a list of phrases for the next time you find yourself in Paris — or Quebec!

ENGLISH	FRENCH
Do you speak English?	Parlez-vous anglais?
Hello.	Bonjour.
Goodbye.	Au revoir.
How are you?	Comment allez-vous?
I am fine, thank you.	Je suis bon, merci.
How old are you?	Quel âge avez-vous?
My name is ____.	Je m'appelle ____.
Thank you.	Merci.
What time is it?	Quelle heure est-il?
Where is the ____?	Où est le/la ____?
You're welcome.	De rien.

Just Added

Quiz time: Have all the English words we'll ever need been already invented? Nope. New words are being added to our language all the time (and no, they won't all be on your next vocabulary quiz . . . but you never know!). And older words get new meanings, too. The dictionary is the place where new words and definitions get the official stamp of approval. Here's a list of some of the phrases or words recently added to the *Merriam-Webster's Collegiate Dictionary*.

Bludge   To avoid work or to sponge off someone else.

Brain freeze   A sudden shooting pain in the head caused by eating very cold food.

Cheesed off   Upset or angry (British)

Cybrarian   A person who deals with information on the Web, as opposed to in books.

Dead presidents   Slang term for money.

Def   Very cool.

Deke   Used in sports – to fake out or fool.

Frankenfood   Food that has been changed at the genetic level.

Goth   Rock music marked by dark lyrics; a fan of that music.

Hazmat   Short for *hazardous materials*.

Identity theft   The illegal use of someone else's name or personal information.

Manga   A popular Japanese form of animation.

Mouse potato   A person who spends way, way, way too much time in front of their computer.

Ollie   A trick in skateboarding in which the rider pops the board off the ground.

Supercross   A motorcycle sport in which drivers race on indoor or arena tracks made of dirt.

Unibrow   When a person's eyebrows meet or nearly meet in the middle.

Words AT WORK

You might know some of these word-related terms, but then again, you might not! So here's a handy list of some useful types of words that will make your writing sing and your reading easier.

Antonyms Words that are opposite of one another. EXAMPLES: Big and small; rough and smooth

Homographs Words with the same spelling but different pronunciations and meanings.
EXAMPLES: Bow (the front of a ship) and bow (as in bow and arrow)

Homophones Words with the same pronunciation but different meanings and spellings.
EXAMPLES: To, too, two

Homonyms Words spelled and pronounced the same, but with different meanings.
EXAMPLES: quail (the bird) and quail (to cower in fear)

Synonyms Words that are the same, or nearly the same, in meaning. EXAMPLES: Huge, enormous, gigantic

Oxymorons

No, these are not unintelligent folks breathing heavily. These are phrases whose words seem to contradict each other: jumbo shrimp, working vacation, small fortune. If it's a shrimp, for instance, how can it be jumbo (meaning huge)?

Looking It Up!

Have you ever asked your teacher or your parents what a word means? What do they usually say? That's right: "Look it up!" So when you go to the dictionary, what do you find? This list shows you the parts of a dictionary definition, based on the example of a word that you'll be familiar with: *goofy*.

goofy \gü-fē\ *adj* **goof·i·er**; **-est** (1921): being crazy, ridiculous, or mildly ludicrous: silly— **goof·i·ly** \-fə-lē\ *adv* — **goof·i·ness** \-fē-nəs\ *n*

- The word itself, often in boldface.
- How to pronounce the word; there are lots of funny ways that letters are written in these pronunciations – check the back of the dictionary for a guide, or ask for help!
- The part of speech, such as adjective, noun, verb, etc.
- The word with its suffixes, in this case to make *goofiest*.
- The year the word was first used in this way in English.
- The definition.
- Other forms of the word that are different parts of speech, along with their own pronunciations and parts of speech.

Getting It Started

Who wrote the first dictionary of English? No one's exactly sure, but one candidate is a gent named Robert Cawdrey, who put together a long list of words in 1604. English writer Samuel Johnson's 1755 dictionary is without a doubt the best up to that point. Noah Webster (yup, he was a real guy) published the first American dictionary in 1806.

Sneaky Smack

Here are some fun ideas for sneaky ways to "give someone the business." Always nice to add a vocabulary lesson to your activities on the playground, right? (Note: Say all of these with a smile on your face!)

"Wow, Joan, that perfume you're wearing is perfectly odoriferous!"
(*Odoriferous* means it smells bad.)

"Nice going, Bob. Your halitosis is really working well today."
(*Halitosis* is a word that means bad breath.)

"Gee, Dan, I wish I could be a great ruminant like you."
(Use this on someone chewing gum; a *ruminant* is an animal, such as a cow, that chews its cud.)

"Ha-ha, that's a good one. Your jokes always make me somnambulate."
(*Somnambulate* means to sleepwalk.)

"That dress you're wearing has a real consanguinity with one my grandma wore."
(*Consanguinity* means having a close relation or connection to.)

Q's Without U's

One of the most famous spelling rules is that the letter Q is always followed by the letter U. Well, we're here to tell you that rule was made to be broken! As any good Scrabble player knows, there are dozens of words that have a Q in them that is *not* followed by a U. Most come from other languages, such as Arabic or Chinese, but have been accepted into some English or Scrabble dictionaries. Here's a short list of rule-breaking words.

Burqa
A garment worn by some Muslim women that covers the face and body

Qadi
A Muslim judge

Qaid
A type of government official in Muslim countries

Qat
A type of shrub found in the Middle East

Qintar
The name of the money used in Albania

Qiviut
The wool on the underside of a musk ox

Qoph
The 19th letter of the Hebrew alphabet

Qwerty
The layout of standard computer keyboards and typewriters

Tranqs
Short for tranquilizers, special drugs that help patients sleep

Umiaq
A word from the Inuit that means "kayak"

How 2 Txt Msg

IMHO, text messaging has become an enormous worldwide communications phenomenon. Billions of text messages are sent around the world — and across the classroom. Most are sent by cell phones, but people can also use other small handheld devices. With a tiny screen and even tinier keys, cell phones are not cut out for writing really long letters. A system of abbreviations has developed to make texting easier and faster. These are different from the "emoticons," or little faces that people make out of various punctuation marks. Here are some of the most well-known text-only abbreviations.

AFAIK	As far as I know
B4	Before
BCNU	Be seein' you
BRB	Be right back
CM	Call me
F2F	Face to face
IMHO	In my humble opinion
JK	Just kidding
L8R	Later
LOL	Laughing out loud
OBTW	Oh, by the way
ROTFL	Rolling on the floor laughing
T+	Think positive
TTFN	Ta-ta for now
TX	Thanks
WTG	Way to go!

Everybody Say "Oki!"

There are more than 50 Aboriginal languages spoken in Canada today. Here are greetings in a few of the most-widely spoken of those languages.

LANGUAGE   GREETING ("HELLO")/PRONUNCIATION

Cree   **tansi**/dahn-say

Ojibwe   **aaniin**/ahh-neen

Mi'kmaq   **kwe**/k-way

Blackfoot   **oki**/oh-kee

Dene   **wotziye**/wot-zee-yeh

Dakota   **hau/han**/how/hahn

Super
Search Tricks

Using a search engine on the Internet is a great way to find information you need (or to find that video of the kid with a pie on his head or something). But there's more to using a search engine than just typing in a word or two. Here are some tips that work on most search engines and can help you find what you need more quickly and more accurately. Make sure it's okay with your folks before you start working on the Internet.

Books

The Google® site has millions of books in its servers. Type in *book* followed by your search term.

Calculator

Either from the search engine's main page or as the top answer to searching this word, you should get to a site that works like a regular desktop calculator. You can also, on some engines, type in a calculation and it will figure it for you.

Conversion

While we hope you use the chart on page 116, you can use search engines to convert imperial to metric measurements (and vice versa) or convert currencies. Type in something like "47 in. in cm" and you'll get 47 in. = 119.38 cm.

Hyphen

Want to eliminate some search results? Use the "-" symbol. For example, if you wanted to look for sites relating to Turkey the nation and not turkey the oh-so-tasty bird, you could type in "turkey -Thanksgiving" or "turkey -bird."

Intitle

Put the word *intitle* before your search term, and what you'll get are only Web sites with that term as part of the title. Using *intext* instead searches for the term in the page, not in the Web site title.

Phone listings

Need to find a friend's phone number? Try typing their name (or family name) and address into the search box; if they have a listed number, it should come up.
On some engines, you need to type *phonebook:* before the name.

Q&A

Find quick answers to basic questions by just asking the question. The answer will come first and include the place where they got it. Type in "population of Greenland," and you'll get "56,375" and perhaps a link to the CIA World Fact Book to check it.

Spelling/Definition

Type the word as best you can (*busines*, for example) and hit search. In most engines, the proper spelling will come up with something like "Did you mean 'business'?" Or type in *define* followed by the word and a definition will come up.

Weather

Type *weather* before a city or location and you'll get a forecast for that area.

Words
Game Page

We'll go with a classic here — a crossword puzzle. You know the drill; read the clues and fill in the blanks. You can find answers to most of the clues within the chapter if you get stuck.

Across

1. Football term for going around something

5. One of the shortest popular verbs

7. What a word means

10. New dictionary word for mutated food

11. Greek word for a place to sweat

Down

2. Where the words live

3. Good _____

4. Slang term for bathroom

6. Slang term for bathroom, or "kick the _____"

8. Super short popular word

9. A "loo" is a bath_____

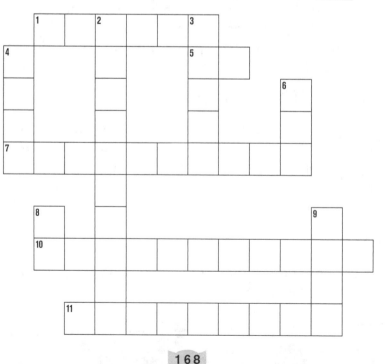

CHAPTER SIX

Pop Culture

What is pop culture? Pretty much everything except homework. If you can watch it, read it, listen to it, dance to it, download it, or just stare at it, you might find it in here.

BEFORE
You Heard of Them

Many entertainers got their first big break in show business in typical ways. For instance, Jennifer Lopez got her start as a dancer on the TV show *In Living Color*. Britney Spears, Justin Timberlake, and Christina Aguilera all wore Mouseketeer ears on *The Mickey Mouse Club* before they became world famous. But for lots of stars, their first jobs had nothing to do with "showbiz." Look at this list of first jobs of the rich and famous.

CELEB	FIRST JOB
Jennifer Aniston	Waitress
Garth Brooks	Boot salesman
Mariah Carey	Hat checker
Jim Carrey	Factory worker
Coolio	Firefighter
Danny DeVito	Hairdresser
Harrison Ford	Carpenter
Faith Hill	Secretary
Madonna	Dunkin' Donuts counter girl
Demi Moore	Debt collector
Jack Nicholson	Mail sorter
Brad Pitt	Refrigerator mover
Jerry Seinfeld	Lightbulb salesman
Robin Williams	Street mime

Great Song, Curtis!

Curtis James Jackson III is one of the world's most popular hip-hop stars. Christopher Bridges sells tons of CDs and makes fans go crazy. Dana Owens is a musical and movie star. What do you *mean* you've never heard of any of these folks? Well, you have, just not by those names. Most rap and hip-hop stars go by childhood nicknames earned before they were famous. Why use the nicknames? Because Clifford and Cornell and Kimberly just don't sound phat.

RAP NAME	REAL NAME
Coolio	Artis Ivey, Jr.
Dr. Dre	Andre Romel Young
Eminem	Marshall Bruce Mathers
Fifty Cent	Curtis James Jackson III
Ice Cube	Oshea Jackson
Jay-Z	Shawn Corey Carter
Lil' Kim	Kimberly Denise Jones
Lil Wayne	Dwayne Michael Carter Jr.
Ludacris	Christopher Bridges
Nelly	Cornell Hayes, Jr.
Puff Daddy (a.k.a. Diddy)	Sean John Combs
Queen Latifah	Dana Owens
Snoop Dogg	Cordazer Calvin Broadus
T.I.	Clifford Harris, Jr.

Juno Awards

Each year, Canadians tip their hats to the Juno winners — our top music awards. Here is a list of the winners for the past five years in the categories of Artist of the Year, Group of the Year, and Album of the Year.

ARTIST OF THE YEAR

2008	Feist
2007	Nelly Furtado
2006	Michael Bublé
2005	Avril Lavigne
2004	Sam Roberts

GROUP OF THE YEAR

2008	Blue Rodeo
2007	Billy Talent
2006	Nickelback
2005	Billy Talent
2004	Nickelback

ALBUM OF THE YEAR

2008	The Reminder (Feist)
2007	Loose (Nelly Furtado)
2006	It's Time (Michael Bublé)
2005	Billy Talent (Billy Talent)
2004	We Were Born In A Flame (Sam Roberts)

Hall of Famers

The Canadian Music Hall of Fame recognizes artists who have made outstanding contributions to our country's music industry. Here are the inductees for the last decade.

YEAR	ARTIST
2008	Triumph
2007	Bob Rock
2006	Bryan Adams
2005	The Tragically Hip
2004	Bob Ezrin
2003	Tom Cochrane
2002	Daniel Lanois
2001	Bruce Cockburn
2000	Bruce Fairbairn
1999	Luc Plamondon
1998	David Foster

No. 1 in No. 1s

It's a big deal to get to the No. 1 spot on *Billboard Magazine*'s Hot 100 chart, and very few artists have done it more than once. Even fewer have done it more than ten times. And once you're up there, it's hard to stay. Here are some singers who have done it. This list covers songs released from January 1, 1955 to the present.

Artists with the Most No. 1 Hits

The Beatles	20
Mariah Carey	18
Michael Jackson	13
The Supremes	12
Madonna	12
Whitney Houston	11
Janet Jackson	10

Artists with the Most Weeks at No. 1

Mariah Carey	89 weeks
The Beatles	59 weeks
Boyz II Men	50 weeks
Usher	43 weeks
Michael Jackson	37 weeks
Elton John	34 weeks

How CDs Are Made

What's as thin as a stick of gum but holds more than an hour of music? A CD, of course. That little plastic disc is just 1.2 mm (.04 in.) thick. How do they get all that stuff onto something so thin? The answer is that every CD has five layers. Here's what they are and what they do.

1 An injection-molded clear polycarbonate plastic layer accounts for the majority of the CD's thickness and weight. It protects the data layer from damage on the play side, and also acts as a lens to focus the CD player's laser onto the data layer.

2 The clear plastic layer is molded or pressed with microscopic bumps arranged as a single, continuous, extremely long spiral track. This is the data layer, where the music and any other information is stored. It's the layer that the CD player reads.

3 A thin, reflective aluminum layer lies on top of the data layer. It acts like a mirror. The CD player shines a laser onto the data bumps; the light is reflected back to the detector in the CD player by this shiny layer.

4 An ultra-thin plastic coating is added to protect the reflective and data layers. It also forms a surface for the label layer.

5 The label layer is printed on top of the protective layer. This is the part that tells you what's on the CD.

How Big Is a Bump?

The spiral track on the data layer circles from the inside of the disc to the outside. The elongated bumps that make up the track are each about 0.5 microns wide (a micron is a millionth of a metre) and 125 nanometres high (a nanometre is a billionth of a metre). That's incredibly tiny, but the track itself is very long. If you could lift the data track off a CD and stretch it out, it would be almost 5 km (3.5 miles) long!

With the Band

When large rock, hip-hop, or country groups go out on tour, they take along a bunch of helpers called "roadies" (short for road crew). Roadies travel with the musicians and handle every part of the tour and the show except for actually playing the music. They often do a lot of different things, but some roadies have very specific jobs. Here are a few of them.

FOH engineer FOH stands for "front of house." This is the sound technician who sits out in the audience, often behind a big electronics board, adjusting all the speakers, amps, and microphones so they sound just right.

Guitar tech This is the only person who is allowed to handle a musician's guitars. He orders supplies such as picks and strings; maintains and repairs guitars, amplifiers, and cables; restrings, cleans, and tunes the guitars; sets up all the guitars and their equipment on the stage; and retunes or restrings a guitar during a performance, if necessary.

Instrument techs Bass players, drummers, and keyboard players may also have technicians whose only job is to keep the instruments working properly and make sure they are set up onstage. This can include details like making sure a special lucky stuffed animal is sitting in a certain place on a certain keyboard.

Lighting techs Lighting technicians are involved with setting up and controlling lighting equipment for the club or arena where the band plays.

Pyrotechnics/SFX Explosions, flashes, smoke, or flames on stage are called pyrotechnics, and these guys set them all up. SFX stands for "special effects," and the SFX guys may also coordinate with the lighting techs and the stage manager for other kinds of special effects.

Security Keeping the musicians safe and making sure nobody barges in on them is the main job of these guys. They also make sure no one gets up on the stage during a concert.

Sound techs These guys set up, test, and operate the sound equipment, and select, place, and adjust microphones. They may also operate controls to maintain correct sound levels and introduce prerecorded special effects during the show.

Stage manager The stage manager organizes the concert, making sure all the other roadies and technicians know what their jobs are.

Steel dogs This is the crew that builds those tall steel towers for shows at stadiums.

Tour manager This person organizes the schedule the group will follow, including what venues they will play at, who will go along with the band, what hotels they'll stay at, and how they will get from place to place.

Truss spotlight operators These are the guys who sit in the lighting truss (a set of pipes and brackets that hold up the many lights) above the stage with a safety belt holding them in their chairs. They hit the performers with a spotlight from above and behind.

Get a Grip!

In a movie, the producer, the director, the actors — and sometimes the costume designers — get all the attention and win all the Oscars. But there are a lot of other cool movie jobs that won't make you famous. Here are some of them.

Best boy The second person in charge of any group on set, most commonly the chief assistant to the gaffer (see below); women can be best boys.

Body double Takes the place of the actor for a specific scene, usually because their body has a characteristic that the actor lacks, such as big muscles or pretty feet.

Boom operator Holds the boom microphone (a microphone attached to the end of a long pole) out over the actors.

Camera loader Operates the clapboard, signalling the beginning of a shot, and also loads the film into the film magazines.

Continuity coordinator Takes photographs of every scene to make sure the actors always are wearing the right clothing or have the right props the next time a similar scene is shot.

Dialogue coach Helps an actor's speech fit their character, usually by assisting with pronunciation and accents.

Foley artist Creates incidental sound effects, such as footsteps and other noises, in a film.

Gaffer In charge of the electrical department.

Grip Maintains and positions equipment on a set; the dolly grip positions the small truck that rolls along tracks and carries the camera, cameraperson, and occasionally the director; the key grip is in charge of a group of grips.

Wrangler Responsible for the care and control of all animals on the set; there are also "baby wranglers," who help keep track of child or infant actors.

Dig These DVDs

Don't you just love to see a great movie over and over? The fact that you know what happens next and what everyone is going to say is part of the fun. These were the top ten bestselling movies on DVD in 2008 (from Amazon.com; PG-13 and below).

1 *The Dark Knight*

2 *John Adams*

3 *Iron Man*

4 *Indiana Jones and the Kingdom of the Crystal Skull*

5 *Sleeping Beauty: Special Edition*

6 *National Treasure 2*

7 *Mamma Mia!*

8 *Transformers*

9 *Batman Begins*

10 *Wall-E*

Spy Guys & Gals

Some of the most popular — and coolest! — characters in movies and on TV are spies! Their exploits amaze and entertain us — and sometimes make us laugh. They have the best "toys," they drive the coolest cars, and they sneak into the most sneakproof places. Through it all, they remain smooth and easygoing. We asked an expert on movie and TV spies to give us a list of ten of the most popular, most fun, coolest movie and TV spies of all time.

1. James Bond

Getting his gadgets from Q and his assignments from M, British Agent 007 — cinema's most famous spy — has saved the world from criminal masterminds in 22 movies since 1962. Six actors have played Bond on the big screen.

2. Austin Powers

A satire of James Bond, Mike Myers's comic spy Austin Powers was frozen in the 1960s so he could be defrosted in the 1990s to defeat the criminal plans of Dr. Evil. Myers played both characters in three Austin Powers movies (1997–2002).

3. The Spy Kids

Carmen and Juni Cortez are young spies who helped their secret-agent parents battle evildoers in three *Spy Kids* adventure films (2001–03).

4. The Impossible Missions Force

Jim Phelps is the master spy who, with his team of specialists, carried out "impossible missions" for the U.S. government in the CBS-TV series *Mission: Impossible* (1966–73). Decades later, Tom Cruise produced and starred in three feature films loosely based on this hit spy show.

5. Napoleon Solo & Illya Kuryakin

These cool spies were once as popular as The Beatles. Solo and Illya were agents on *The Man From U.N.C.L.E.*, and, from 1964 to 1968 on NBC, they battled Thrush, a worldwide conspiracy intent on taking over the world.

7. Cody Banks

In the *Agent Cody Banks* movies (2003–04), Frankie Muniz played a teenage kid who is recruited by the CIA to use his skateboarding and snowboarding skills – along with some cool gadgets – to carry out secret missions.

8. Maxwell Smart & Agent 99

In the classic TV comedy *Get Smart* (1965–70), Max was the bumbling Agent 86 who, with the beautiful Agent 99, carried out assignments for the Chief of Control to stop the mean and rotten spies of Kaos. Every time Max messed up, you could be sure he'd say, "Sorry about that, Chief!" – a phrase that became popular all over North America.

9. James West & Artemus Gordon

On the clever CBS-TV series *The Wild Wild West* (1965–69), U.S. Secret Service agents West and Gordon used gadgets, disguises, and their private train to battle villains in the days of the American West.
The show was remade into a movie starring Will Smith in 1999.

10. Kelly Robinson & Alexander Scott

In the groundbreaking NBC-TV show *I Spy* (1965–68), Kelly and Scott were U.S. agents who carried out their undercover missions by travelling the world as a tennis player and his trainer. The first North American TV series to co-star an African-American (Bill Cosby), *I Spy* was remade in 2002 into a comedy film starring Eddie Murphy and Owen Wilson.

CELEBRITY
Kids' Book Authors

Madonna has done it fourteen times and Jamie Lee Curtis has done it eight. NFL stars have done it along with country music singers. What are they all doing? Writing children's books. It's become a hot thing among celebrities to write kids' books. Here are some celebrities who have published books for little kids.

Jason Alexander — *Dad, Are You the Tooth Fairy?*

Tiki Barber and Ronde Barber — *By My Brother's Side*

Katie Couric — *The Blue Ribbon Day, The Brand New Kid*

Billy Crystal — *I Already Know I Love You*

Jamie Lee Curtis — *Today I Feel Silly, Is There Really a Human Race?, I'm Gonna Like Me, Where Do Balloons Go?, It's Hard to be Five, When I Was Little, Tell Me Again About the Night I Was Born*

Whoopi Goldberg — *Alice*

Mia Hamm — *Winners Never Quit!*

Jay Leno — *If Roast Beef Could Fly*

John Lithgow — *I'm a Manatee, The Remarkable Farkle McBride, Marsupial Sue, Carnival of the Animals*

Madonna — *The English Roses* Series, *Lotsa de Casha, The Adventures of Abdi, Mr. Peabody's Apples, Yakov and the Seven Thieves*

Dolly Parton — *Coat of Many Colors*

Jerry Seinfeld — *Halloween*

John Travolta — *Propeller One-Way Night Coach*

Kid Authors

The classic story *Frankenstein* was written in 1818 by Mary Shelley when she was just 19 years old. But she was certainly not the youngest person to write a book. If you like to write, think about these kids who wrote books when they were even younger than Shelley. We'd love to have you on this list next time we get around to updating this book!

Gil C. Alicea/16
The Air Down Here: True Tales From a South Bronx Boyhood

Amelia Atwater-Rhodes/13
In the Forests of the Night

Charlotte Brontë/13
The Search After Happiness

Zlata Filipovic/13
Zlata's Diary: A Child's Life in Wartime Sarajevo

Anne Frank/14
Diary of a Young Girl

Alec Grevin/9
How to Talk to Girls

Latoya Hunter/12
Diary of Latoya Hunter: My First Year in Junior High

S.E. Hinton/16
The Outsiders

Gordon Korman/12
This Can't Be Happening at Macdonald Hall!

Megan McNeil Libby/16
Postcards From France

Dave Lindsay/14
Dave's Quick and Easy Web Pages

Christopher Paolini/15
Eragon

Who's Who in

If you read *Harry Potter and the Philosopher's Stone*, *The Chamber of Secrets*, *The Prisoner of Azkaban*, *The Goblet of Fire*, *The Order of the Phoenix*, *The Half-Blood Prince*, and *The Deathly Hallows*, you know the wizarding universe has grown pretty large. Here's a handy guide to the major characters.

The Potters

Harry Potter
James and Lily Potter, Harry's parents
Vernon and Petunia Dursley, Harry's muggle uncle and aunt
Dudley Dursley, Harry's muggle cousin

Harry's School Friends

Ron Weasley
Hermione Granger
Neville Longbottom
Parvati Patil
Padma Patil

Luna Lovegood
Fred Weasley
George Weasley
Ginny Weasley

Harry's School Enemies

Draco Malfoy   Vincent Crabbe   Gregory Goyle

Hogwarts Teachers

Albus Dumbledore, headmaster
Filius Flitwick, charms
Minerva McGonagall, transfiguration
Horace Slughorn, potions
Severus Snape, potions, defense against the dark arts
Pomona Sprout, herbology
Gilderoy Lockhart, defense against the dark arts

Harry Potter

Argus Filch, caretaker
Rubeus Hagrid, care of magical creatures
Madam Hooch, flying
Aurora Sinistra, astronomy
Sybill Patricia Trelawney, divination
Wilhelmina Grubbly-Plank, care of magical creatures

Other Wizards

Sirius Black, Order of the Phoenix
Remus Lupin, Order of the Phoenix
Alastor Moody, Order of the Phoenix
Lord Voldemort (real name Tom Marvolo Riddle)
Bellatrix Lestrange, follower of Voldemort
Lucius Malfoy, follower of Voldemort
Peter Pettigrew, follower of Voldemort
Dolores Umbridge, unpleasant witch
Quirinus Quirrell, follower of Voldemort
Cornelius Fudge, Minister of Magic
Rufus Scrimgeour, Minister of Magic
Arthur and Molly Weasley, Ron's parents
Charlie, Bill, and Percy Weasley, Ron's grown brothers

Other Creatures

Dobby, house-elf at Hogwarts
Kreacher, house-elf at Hogwarts
Hedwig, Harry's owl
Pigwidgeon, Ron's owl

Crookshanks, Hermione's cat
Mrs. Norris, Argus Filch's cat
Scabbers, Ron's rat

Cell Phone Stuff

Among the more than 3 billion people with cell phones in the world are more than 17 million Canadians. However, Canada's 52 cell phone subscribers for every 100 residents, is far below places like England or Finland, which are nearly 100 for 100! Here are some other facts about cell phones and the role they play in Canadian lives.

* 52 percent of Canadian teens have their own cell phone.

* People from 13 to 24 are the largest group of cell phone users in Canada.

* 93 percent of Canadian teens with cell phones use text messaging every day.

* Thanks to cell phones, teens' use of Internet chat is down from 75 percent to less than 30 percent.

* The number of text messages sent annually by Canadians jumped from 173 million in 2002 to 1.8 billion by 2008!

Cell phones have grown faster than almost any technology in history. In 2000, only about 100 million people had cell phones. Nine years later, more than half the people in the *world* have one. More and more people are giving up their regular land lines and going "all-cell."

Star Barkers

Snoop Dogg keeps Siamese cats. Other celebrity cat lovers include Regis Philbin, Martha Stewart, Kirsten Dunst, Jay Leno, Christina Ricci, Leeza Gibbons, Billy Crystal, and Lisa Loeb. Matt LeBlanc has a pet lizard, and Jacob Underwood from O-Town has a monkey named Abbey. But by far the most visible and most popular celebrity pets are dogs. And when it comes to dogs, those tiny Chihuahuas are really big. Here are some canines of the rich and famous.

CELEBRITY	DOG
Jessica Alba	2 Pugs
Jessica Biel	Bulldog
Jim Carrey	Great Dane
Hilary Duff	Chihuahua
David Duchovny	Collie-Terrier mix
Brett Favre	Yorkshire Terrier
Wayne Gretzky	Dachshund
Janet Jackson	Chow Chow, Mixed breed
Ashley Judd	Cockapoo
Stephen King	Pembroke Welsh Corgi
Jude Law	Mixed breed
Madonna	Chihuahua
Kelly Osborne	Puggle
Pink	Mixed breed
Adam Sandler	Bulldog
Jessica Simpson	Maltipoo
Will Smith	2 Rottweilers
Britney Spears	Chihuahua
Oprah Winfrey	2 Amer. Cocker Spaniels
Kristi Yamaguchi	Toy Rat Terrier

Kids' Choice Champs

People don't ask kids what they think about stuff nearly enough. One exception is Nickelodeon; every year, the cable TV network asks kids to vote for their favourite movies, TV shows, music, and famous people. In 2008, they had their 21st annual Kids' Choice Awards. The show always features lots of celebrity guests, musical acts (New Kids on the Block — trust us, they were famous at the time — provided the first musical performance for a Kids' Choice Awards show), and plenty of slime.

CATEGORY	2008 WINNERS
TV Show	*Drake & Josh*
Reality Show	*American Idol*
TV Actress	Miley Cyrus
TV Actor	Drake Bell
Movie	*Alvin and the Chipmunks*
Movie Actor	Johnny Depp
Movie Actress	Jessica Alba
Animated Movie	*Ratatouille*

Voice from an Animated Movie

Eddie Murphy *(Shrek the Third)*

CATEGORY	2008 WINNERS
Cartoon	*Avatar: The Last Airbender*
Male Athlete	**Tony Hawk**
Female Athlete	**Danica Patrick**
Female Singer	**Miley Cyrus**
Male Singer	**Chris Brown**
Music Group	**The Jonas Brothers**
Song	**"Girlfriend" (Avril Lavigne)**
Book Series	*Harry Potter Series*
Video Game	**Madden NFL '08**

The Wannabe Award

The Wannabe Award is given every year to the celebrity kids most want to be like. Here are some recent winners:

1997	Will Smith	2003	Will Smith
1998	Tia & Tamera Mowry	2004	Adam Sandler
1999	Jonathan Taylor Thomas	2005	Queen Latifah
2000	Rosie O'Donnell	2006	Chris Rock
2001	Tom Cruise	2007	Ben Stiller
2002	Janet Jackson	2008	Cameron Diaz

Canadian TV

Many shows on TV today are Canadian-made: *Corner Gas, Little Mosque on the Prairie, The Rick Mercer Show, Life With Derek, Naturally Sadie, The Nature of Things.* Not to mention popular talent competitions like *So You Think You Can Dance Canada* and *Canadian Idol.* Some Canadian shows are not only well-known here, but in other countries too. Here are some of the shows that "made it" in the U.S.

Degrassi Junior High/ Degrassi High

SCTV

Hockey Night in Canada

Trailer Park Boys

Kids in the Hall

This Hour Has 22 Minutes

Today's Special

You Can't Do That On Television

The Red Green Show

The Newsroom

Cool Cartoons

What goes better with Saturday morning than cartoons? Of course, cartoons go pretty well with just about any morning . . . or afternoon . . . or evening. These are the most popular animated shows (for kids) in 2008, according to TV.com.

SHOW NAME	FIRST YEAR ON AIR
1. *Naruto*	2002
2. *Avatar: The Last Airbender*	2005
3. *Ben 10: Alien Force*	2008
4. *SpongeBob SquarePants*	1999
5. *Total Drama Island*	2007
6. *Star Wars: Clone Wars*	2005
7. *Digimon: Digital Monsters*	1999
8. *Yu-Gi-Oh GX*	2005
9. *Justice League Unlimited*	2001
10. *The Fairly OddParents*	2001

? What did Stephen Hillenburg, the creator of SpongeBob SquarePants, study in college? Well, he did study some art, but he was also a student of natural resource planning with a main interest in oceanography and marine biology. Glub, glub!

Who's Who in
The Simpsons

The Simpsons began life in 1987 as one-minute cartoons on *The Tracey Ullman Show*. They were created by cartoonist Matt Groening, and became a weekly series in 1989. Now, *The Simpsons* is the longest-running animated series in the history of television. A lot of characters have come and gone in all those years. Here are some of them.

The Simpson Family

Homer Simpson, father

Marge Simpson, mother

Bart Simpson, son

Lisa Simpson, daughter

Maggie Simpson, baby daughter

Abe and Mona Simpson, Homer's parents

Jacqueline and Clancy Bouvier, Marge's parents

Selma and Patty Bouvier, Marge's twin sisters

Springfield Residents

Comic Book Guy, owner, Android's Dungeon

Charles Montgomery "Monty" Burns, owner of Springfield Nuclear Power Plant

Carl Carlson, Homer's coworker

Ned Flanders, Simpsons' next-door neighbor

Rod and Todd, Ned's sons

Groundskeeper Willie, school groundskeeper

Barney Gumble, regular at Moe's Tavern

Dr. Julius Hibbert, physician

Edna Krabappel, fourth-grade teacher

Krusty the Klown, TV celebrity

Lenny Leonard, Homer's coworker

Timothy Lovejoy, reverend of First Church of Springfield

Nelson Muntz, school bully

Apu Nahasapeemapetilon, owns the Kwik-E-Mart

Manjula Nahasapeemapetilon, Apu's wife

Poonam, Sashi, Pria, Uma, Anoop, Sandeep, Nabendu, Gheet, the Nahasapeemapetilon children

Sherri and Terri, purple-haired twins

Seymour Skinner, Springfield Elementary School principal

Agnes Skinner, Seymour's mother

Waylon Smithers, Jr., Mr. Burns's assistant

Cletus and Brandine Delroy, country folks

Mo Szyslak, owner of Moe's Tavern

Milhouse Van Houten, Bart's best friend

Clancy Wiggum, chief of police

Ralph Wiggum, school idiot

? Matt Groening's real father is named Homer and his mother is named Margaret. He also has two sisters, Lisa and Maggie. He says he named the main character Bart because it is an anagram of *brat*. What's an anagram? It's a word made by mixing up the letters of another word.

TV Firsts

We know, we know . . . you don't watch a lot of TV. You're a reader, an athlete, an artist . . . you don't need the boob tube. Yeah . . . right. C'mon, admit it: you love TV. We do! (Though we shouldn't overdo it.) We could probably do a whole book on lists of TV things like shows, actors, awards, etc. But here we'll flick the switch to TV history and give you this list of cool TV firsts, without which you'd just be staring at an empty box instead of a TV (and with some of the stuff on TV these days, an empty box might be better!).

First TV broadcast J. L. Baird and Charles Jenkins combined their own work with that of earlier inventors (such as Karl Braun and Paul Nipkow) to transmit the first (fuzzy!) pictures in 1926.

First workable TV transmission device Philo T. Farnsworth built on the work of other scientists and added his own twists to land a spot as the "inventor" of television, with the creation of his machine in 1930.

First TV program This unnamed show of music, speeches, and comics was aired on July 21, 1931.

First TV in Canada Alphonse Ouimet built it in 1932. By 1947, he was in charge of starting Canada's first television network – in English and French!

First successful colour TV This was invented in 1941 by scientists at Bell Labs. *Walt Disney's World of Color* was the first colour TV show, in 1961.

First TV dinner Dig in and watch! The Swanson Company first sold these in 1953.

First remote control Thank goodness! Couch potatoes everywhere rejoiced when Robert Adler invented this in 1956.

First satellite dish Taylor Howard invented this device in 1976.

First DVDs Several companies combined to produce these for the first time in 1995.

POPULAR
Video Games

There are so many video games and video-game platforms out there that you'd need a school full of kids to play them all. There's no way one person could (or should!) play all these games. But video games are part of many kids' lives. The key is to make sure that they're *part* of your life . . . not all of it! Here are some video games that many experts recommend as good ones for kids.

Disney Friends

Hannah Montana: Music Jam

Lego Star Wars

Mario Strikers Charged

Nancy Drew:
Legend of the Crystal Skull

Patapon

Pokémon Red, Blue, and Green

Rock Band Special Edition

Super Mario Brothers.

Super Mario Galaxy

Wii Sports

Zack and Wiki:
Quest for Barbaros' Treasure

Pop Culture
Game Page

Okay, we need your help. There's been a massive computer glitch at a gigantic pop culture Web site. Dozens of superstars' names have been mixed up in horrible ways. You need to unscramble the names below (all found in this chapter) and then take the first letters of the resulting names and put them, in order, in the blanks at the bottom to form the mystery word at the bottom (the source of the computer bug, as it turns out).

LEAEBTS   _____

TUASIN REWOPS   _____   _____

NRIBO LLAWMIIS   _____   _____

IIKT ERRBAB   _____   _____

VESRSUE PAENS   _____   _____

EIC EUCB   _____   _____

EXLLWAM ASRTM   _____

KNPI   _____

EPSTHNE GINK   _____   _____

HAORP WRIENYF   _____   _____

NYACN WRDE   _____   _____

Answer: __ __ __ __   __ __ __ __ __

CHAPTER SEVEN

Animals

Sure, we've got some of the "usual" animals in here, like dogs (ugly ones) and horses (including some from Xilingol). But we've also got poisonous lizards, bugs the size of your hand, and waterskiing squirrels.
Be an animal . . . and dig in!

The Top Dogs

Hundreds of dog breeds live all over the world — but they came from different places. The silky-coated Afghan Hound, for example, originated in Afghanistan. Can you guess where these terrier breeds come from: Irish Terrier, Australian Terrier, Black Russian Terrier, Boston Terrier, Welsh Terrier, Tibetan Terrier, Irish Terrier, and Scottish Terrier? Too easy? How about the dog breeds listed below? (Um, here's a hint: They're all from Canada . . .)

Canadian Inuit dog

Labrador retriever

Landseer

Mackenzie River husky

Newfoundland

Nova Scotia duck-tolling retriever

St. John's water dog

Seppala Siberian sled dog

Valley bulldog

Ugly Dog WINNERS

Not every dog is a cute and cuddly puppy. Some of them are downright ugly. Ugly, that is, to everyone but their loving owners. All in the spirit of fun, numerous "ugly dog" contests are held each year. Here are stories about some of the winners.

Sam, a nearly hairless Chinese Crested with crooked teeth and wrinkly skin, was the most famous "ugly dog" in the world until his death at age 14 in 2005. He won contests around the world and appeared on numerous TV shows.

Hoss was the three-time winner of a contest in North Carolina. He was a mix of Labrador Retriever and Basset Hound, but what made him, well, unique? According to one newspaper, it was "an underbite that makes his bottom teeth stick out like a barracuda."

Sushi, a Japanese Chin mix, won a radio station contest in Medford, Massachusetts. Her wrinkly brown skin, mismatched eyes, and blunt snout wowed (or grossed out) the judges.

Zippy was another Chinese Crested who had a habit of sticking her tongue out the side of her mouth. She won a pile of ugly dog contests and was featured on TV, in books, and on calendars.

MOST POPULAR
Pet Names

See Spot run. See Spot sit. See Spot complain that his name is too boring and that he wants a new one! Here's a list of some alternatives for naming your dog or cat. These are the most popular names, based on how often the name has been put on a pet tag.

Max
Jake
Buddy
Maggie
Bear
Molly
Bailey
Shadow
Sam
Lady

Sadie
Lucky
Rocky
Lucy
Daisy
Buster
Casey
Cody
Brandy
Duke

Unusual Pets

There are about 3.5 million pet dogs in Canada and about 4.5 million pet cats. And don't forget about a gazillion pet fish. But those are everyday pets, pets everyone has seen or, well, petted (except maybe the fish). Here's a list of real animals that some people (okay, maybe just a few people) keep as pets. Ask your mom and dad to check these out!

African giant millipedes

African pygmy hedgehogs

Chinchillas

Ferrets

Hermit crabs

Madagascar hissing cockroaches

Potbellied pigs

Prairie dogs

Stick insects

Tarantulas

Tree frogs

Exotic Tips

Pets like these are known as "exotic" pets, and they need some special care. Here are a few random tips about living with some of these animals: • Ferrets can be litter-box-trained like cats. • You have to trim the tusks of potbellied pigs. • Don't pick a hedgehog up from the top. • Hissing cockroaches eat crushed dry dog or cat food; put Vaseline on the edge of an aquarium so they can't get out.

Famous Canadians and
Their Pets

Even famous people could use a furry best friend sometimes. Here are some well-known Canadians and their well-loved pets.

Alexander Graham Bell had a pet terrier named Trouve, whose barks he used to help him learn about sound.

Famous west coast artist and writer **Emily Carr** had a pet monkey named Woo. She also had a menagerie of cats, dogs, rabbits, parrots, squirrels, and rats!

Sports commentator and former NHL coach **Don Cherry** has had two English Bull Terriers, both called Blue, that have appeared with him on his hockey videos.

Prime Minister **John Diefenbaker** had a pet dog named Tip. A special stone at Diefenbaker's birthplace, now the site of the Canadian Royal Heritage Museum, marks its burial spot.

Prime Minister **Stephen Harper** has an orange cat named Cheddar. The prime minister and his wife also foster cats that are waiting to be adopted from the Ottawa Humane Society.

Prime Minister **William Lyon Mackenzie King** had an Irish Terrier named Pat. There is even a bronze statue of the former prime minister and his dog.

Three of comedian **Mike Myers'** dogs were named after hockey players: Gilmour, Borschevsky, and 99 (after the jersey number of hockey great Wayne Gretzky — who himself has a pet: a Dachshund named Clyde).

Musician **Sarah McLachlan** has a Labrador Retriever named Rex that appeared in an SPCA commercial with her.

Animals with
Horns

First, a definition: Horns are permanent, bony parts of animals. Antlers, unlike bones, can have forks, or different branches, and they are shed annually. Horns are usually on an animal for life. This list includes animal families — all mammals — from around the world that have horns, and, of course, this means they have a tough time putting sweaters on over their heads. Just kidding . . . this means they have horns that they use in self-defense, as a way to attract mates, or as tools to find food. Don't let anybody horn in on you while you're reading this list!

Antelope
Bison
Cow
Deer
Giraffe
Goat
Narwhal
Rhinoceros
Sheep

Cool fact: Rhinoceros horns are not made of bone, but of tightly compacted hair! Sadly, many rhinos have been killed by poachers who want only the horns, which are sold as souvenirs or as "magic" powder.

Apes & Monkeys

Apes and monkeys are our closest relatives in the animal kingdom, but keeping them straight can be confusing. How do you tell which is which? These lists sort out the species. Then we'll explain a few ways you can tell if an animal is a monkey, an ape, or your little brother or sister.

TYPES OF APES

Bonobo

Chimpanzee

Gibbon

Gorilla

Orangutan

Siamang

TYPES OF MONKEYS

Baboon

Capuchin

Celebes

Colobus

Guenon

Howler

Langur

Macaque

Mandrill

Mangabey

Marmoset

Proboscis

Rhesus

Sake

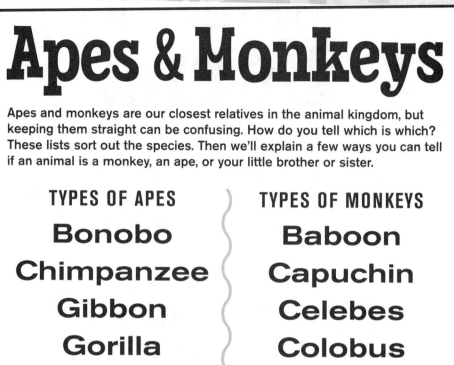

TYPES OF MONKEYS, CONTINUED
Spider
Squirrel
Tamarin
Titi
Uakari
Woolly

Ape or Monkey: What's the Difference?

Apes and monkeys (and humans, too!) are all primates. All have hair, eyes that face front, opposable thumbs, and fingernails instead of claws. But there are some differences. Here's a handy list:

APES	MONKEYS
✔ No tails	✔ Most have tails
✔ Can reach up to grab branches	✔ Can't reach up
✔ Can walk on two feet	✔ Walk only on four feet
✔ May have bare patches on face	✔ Hair all over face
✔ Larger brain	✔ Smaller brain
✔ Some have learned sign language	✔ None have learned sign language

Accidental Tourists

It's fun to pack your bags, get on a ship, plane, or train, and go somewhere new. But when you go, you buy a ticket. When unwanted plants and animals make these trips to Canada, they're sneaking in. The bad news is that when they get here, they can push out native plants and animals, becoming "invasive species." Great measures are needed to control or get rid of them. These plants and animals didn't start out here, but they've moved into various places and are causing a lot of damage.

Asian long-horned beetle

Brown spruce long-horned beetle

Emerald ash borer

European gypsy moth

Garlic mustard

Purple loosestrife

Sea lamprey

Sirex wasp

Starling

Zebra mussel

Pandas
with Passports

As you probably know, the giant panda is native to China. That's the only place in the world where these shy and rare animals live in the wild. However, so many people around the world want to see pandas up close that China lends some of the animals to zoos around the world. As of 2008, these are the giant pandas living outside of China.

PANDAS/ZOO SITE

Lun Lun, Yang Yang, Mei Lan/Atlanta, Georgia

Bao Bao, Yan Yan/Berlin, Germany

Tan Tan, Kou Kou/Kobe, Japan

Ling Ling/Kyoto, Japan

Ya Ya, La La/Memphis, Tennessee

Xiu Hua, Shuang Shuang, Xin Xin/Mexico City, Mexico

Bai Yun, Gao Gao, Su Lin, Mei Sheng/San Diego, California

Mei Mei, Lau Hin/Wakayama, Japan

Mei Xiang, Tian Tian/Washington, D.C.

Note: There may be a giant panda in a zoo in North Korea, but no one knows for sure because that country is mostly closed to visitors.

Big Birds!

Most birds are rather small, usually cute, and tweet a lot. That's not what this list is about, however. This list is about the biggest members of the bird family. These are not songbirds for your backyard feeder; these are the elephants of birdland. (Note: The tall, yellow bird from that popular TV show is not on our list!) Their homes are listed with their names.

Biggest Bird
The ostrich (Africa) is the tallest and heaviest bird. It can weigh about 115–135 kg (240–300 lb.) and stand up to 2.75 m (9 ft.) tall. It also lays the largest eggs in the bird world; one ostrich egg would hold 24 chicken eggs! However, an ostrich can't fly.

Largest Flying Bird
The Kori bustard (Africa) and the great bustard (Europe) somehow get aloft even though they weigh about 18 kg (40 lb.).

Tallest Flying Birds
Some species of cranes, which live in many places around the world, can be as much as 2 m (6 ft., 6 in.) tall.

Widest Wingspan
The mighty albatross (southern hemisphere) has wings that measure — from tip to tip while fully spread — as much as 330 cm (11 ft.).

Biggest Bill
Only birds (and duckbilled platypuses, of course) have bills. The longest bills in the bird world belong to Australian pelicans, whose bills can be up to 45 cm (18 in.) long.

 Okay, once and for all: Do ostriches really stick their heads in the sand? You've probably seen them do it in cartoons, but in real life, they are just putting their heads near the ground to fool far-off predators into thinking that the bushy bird is, well, a bush.

WORLD'S
Rarest Birds

Ornithologists (people who study birds) were thrilled in 2004 when reports came out of Louisiana that an ivory-billed woodpecker had been spotted in a swamp. The bird had not been seen in the wild since 1944 and was believed to be extinct. Here is a list of other extremely rare birds. The population of each of these birds is estimated to be less than 250!

BIRD	MAIN RANGE
Alagoas curassow	Brazil
Bishop's 'o'o	Hawaii
Black-breasted puffin	Ecuador
California condor	California
Chinese crested tern	Asia
Crested ibis	China
Zino's petrel	Madeira
Giant ibis	Cambodia
Gurney's pitta	Malaysia
Imperial Amazon parrot	Dominica
Ivory-billed woodpecker	Louisiana
Jerdon's courser	India
Junin grebe	Peru
Kinglet cotinga	Brazil
Madagascar serpent-eagle	Madagascar
Mauritius parakeet	Mauritius
Rapa fruit-dove	Tahiti
Seychelles magpie-robin	Seychelles
Slender-billed curlew	Russia
Polynesian ground-dove	Moorea
Socorro mockingbird	Mexico
Spix's macaw	Brazil
White-eyed river-martin	Thailand
Yellow-eared parrot	Colombia

Really, Really Poisonous Snakes

First of all, snakes are not slimy. Also, most of them are perfectly harmless to humans. But a list of all the harmless snakes would be boring. This list features some of the most poisonous snakes in the world. Just a few drops of their venom can take down a person or a large animal. We've also included a handy list of their homes . . . so you can stay away from them!

SNAKE	WHERE TO AVOID THEM
Australian brown snake	Australia
Beaked sea snake	Southeast Asia
Black mamba	South America
Boomslang	Africa
Brazilian huntsman	Brazil
Bushmaster	Central and South America
Coral snake	southwest United States
Death adder	Australia, Papua New Guinea
Gabon viper	Africa
Indian cobra	India
Inland taipan	Australia
Malayan krait	Indonesia, Southeast Asia
Mojave rattlesnake	United States/Mexico
Saw-scaled viper	Middle East, North Africa
Tiger snake	Australia

The Gila monster and Mexican beaded lizard are the only poisonous lizards in the world. They live in the southwestern United States and northern Mexico. Please don't step on them.

Big Bugs!

Bugs are not something that you want to be big. Big snacks? Sure. Big pieces of cake? Definitely. Your favourite sports team's score? Of course. But bugs? No . . . you'd probably rather they were small and scarce. However, some insects are just plain big. This is a list of some things that you really hope do not land on your head. (Their homes are listed with their names.)

Heaviest Insect
While not too big compared to, say, a dog, compared to an ant, the goliath beetle (Africa) is a giant! The biggest ones can be almost as big as a tennis ball and weigh 100 g (3.5 oz.).

Longest Insect
The well-named stick insect (Indonesia) can be more than 30 cm (1 ft.) long.

Biggest Moth
The Atlas moth (Asia) has a wingspan of 25-28 cm (10–11 in.), about as big across as your two hands spread out.

Farthest Jumping Insect
The froghopper, or spittlebug, which lives all over the world, can leap up to 71 cm (28 in.), which is 115 times its body length. If you could jump like one, you'd be able to jump to the top of the Calgary Tower.

Biggest Spider
Yes, we know spiders are not insects. They're arachnids. The biggest spider in the world lives in South America. The goliath bird-eating spider is only scary if you're a bird, but it is really huge and can measure 28 cm (11 in.) across!

ONLY IN Australia

As an island continent cut off for centuries by vast oceans, Australia is the home of some of the world's most unique animals. With little contact with the wider world, these animals developed over time into some of the world's most unusual species. There are hundreds of Australia-only snakes, lizards, and insects, but this list is just Aussie mammals. Although these animals are now seen in zoos around the world, Australia remains the only place they call home.

Dingo This is the wild dog of the Australian Outback.

Kangaroo Several species of this large marsupial are found in Australia; they are best known for their large hind legs and jumping ability, and for carrying their young in a pouch.

Koala Another marsupial, this shy, tree-dwelling mammal is cute, fuzzy, and eats only eucalyptus leaves.

Platypus This is the only mammal that lays eggs and has a bird-like bill. It also has a flat tail like a beaver.

Quokka These small marsupials look a bit like large rats with short noses.

Tasmanian devil These small and fierce creatures are the last meat-eating marsupials left in the world.

Wombat Wombats come in several species, but most are small, burrowing, nocturnal animals. The northern hairy-nosed wombat is one of the rarest animals in the world.

Kids' Favourite
Types of Fish

Everyone knows that fish is good for you to eat. It supplies many important nutrients, along with being a good source of protein for energy. So this list is filled with examples of the many foods from the sea that kids love. See if your favourite is on this list.

Tuna

Animals At Work

For thousands of years, animals and humans have worked side by side on farms around the world. Horses carry riders, cows and oxen pull plows, sheep cut grass and share their wool, and chickens lay eggs. But away from the farmyard and the field, animals are hard at work doing other jobs. Here's a list of animals that deserve to earn a paycheque — if only they had pockets to keep their wallets in.

Bloodhounds
These dogs use their supersensitive noses to help track down missing people.

Guide dogs
They assist blind people by helping them get around safely.

Guard geese
At some military installations, geese patrol to help alert the guards to the presence of strangers.

Helper monkeys
Capuchin monkeys work as personal helpers for people in wheelchairs and people with disabilities.

Lab rats
Rats and mice are often used in scientific experiments.

Lumberjack elephants
In India and Thailand, elephants are trained to work with riders to lift heavy logs.

Minesweeper dolphins
Specially trained dolphins help navies search for undersea mines.

Medical maggots
It's kind of gross, but maggots (fly larvae) can be used by doctors to help clean wounds. And yes, they eat the dead flesh!

Police dogs
Working with specially trained officers, K-9 dogs are used to help chase down suspects or to help search for missing people. Other dogs are trained to sniff for explosives or illegal substances.

Truffle pigs
Trained pigs search for valuable truffles, a type of underground fungus somewhat like a mushroom.

Horsin' Around

Among the dozens and dozens of horse breeds from around the world, there is at least one that starts with every letter of the alphabet. Perhaps the most popular breeds are the American Quarter Horse, the American Paint Horse, the Arabian, the Thoroughbred, and the Appaloosa. On this trip through the equine (that means having to do with horses) alphabet, how many have you heard of?

Andalusian

Budyonny

Camargue

Dartmoor pony

Egyptian

Florida cracker

Guangxi

Hanoverian

Icelandic

Jutland

Kisber felver

Lipizzan

Mustang

Norwegian fjörd

Ob

Palomino

Quarab

Racking horse

Shetland pony

Tennessee walking horse

Ukrainian saddle horse

Vlaamperd

Welsh pony

Xilingol

Yakut

Zaniskari pony

Best Zoos
for You

Whether it's the roar of the lions, the antics of the monkeys, or the creepiness of insects, zoo animals provide a fun and enriching experience for people who want to see them close-up. But did you know that zoos do a lot of research into animal health and habits that help animals in the wild, too? Each year the Canadian Association of Zoos and Aquariums rewards the best zoos for their work. These were the 2007 winners.

And the award goes to . . .

. . . the Vancouver Aquarium in Vancouver, British Columbia – Baines Award, for its new learning centre.

. . . the Granby Zoo in Granby, Quebec – Conservation Award, for its "green program."

. . . the African Lion Safari in Cambridge, Ontario – Outstanding Achievement Award, for its giraffe training program.

. . . the Valley Zoo in Edmonton, Alberta – Enrichment Award, for its advancement in lemur care.

America's Best

Child magazine did a survey that looked at all the zoos in the United States. They chose these five as the best "family-friendly" zoos: 1) Lowry Park Zoo/Tampa, Florida, 2) San Diego Zoo/San Diego, California, 3) Oklahoma City Zoological Park and Botanical Garden/Oklahoma City, Oklahoma, 4) Brookfield Zoo/Brookfield, Illinois, 5) Phoenix Zoo/Phoenix, Arizona.

Zoo Food

Your parents have it tough. They have to work hard to buy the good food that keeps you healthy — and they usually have to make it for you, too. But you're just kids — imagine if they had to feed an entire zoo! The kitchen folks at zoos around the world have to do that every day. For instance, the royal python at the Toronto Zoo enjoys 25 g of mice each Wednesday, while the zoo's alligators dine on 225 g of herring on Saturdays. Miami's 175 fruit bats enjoy 1,000 l of peach nectar a year! For a more complete picture, the animal chefs (chefs for animals, that is, not animals as chefs!) at the St. Louis Zoo provided this inside peek at a year's menu for everything from aardvarks to zebras. Their Animal Food and Nutrition Centre staff uses this food and more to feed the hundreds of animals at their zoo.

306 kg of earthworms

1,000 cases of kale

5.4 tons of primate biscuits

18 tons of herring

1.4 tons of squid

4.5 tons of smelt

9 tons of dog food
(for various animals, not for dogs!)

13.6 tons of mackerel

500 cases of bananas

520 cases of apples

9 tons of carrots

70.8 tons of pellets for herbivores
(plant-eaters)

PLUS

675,000 waxworms

22,000 adult mice

13,000 bales of hay

1,625,000 mealworms

260,000 flightless houseflies

1,200,000 crickets

It Takes a Village to Raise a Panda

Lun Lun, a panda at the Atlanta Zoo and a new mom (see page 207), and her "husband" Yang Yang have a lot of help raising their new cub. A trio of keepers spends 70 hours a week just taking care of Yang Yang. Five other keepers, including a panda expert brought in from China, care for Lun Lun and the cub round-the-clock. Four people chop 567 kg (1,250 lb.) of bamboo every week to feed the pandas. That's a lot of "panda pals!"

Amazing Animals

Your dog can do a trick or two, probably. He can sit or roll over or fetch. Maybe you've trained your cat to play with a toy. Big deal! After you read about these real-life animal feats, you'll look at your own pets in a whole new way!

Agatha
Though blind, this "watch cat" attacked and chased away a burglar trying to break into her owner's house.

Buster
A springer spaniel and a member of Great Britain's Royal Army, Buster is trained to sniff out explosives. He located a huge pile of weapons in Iraq and received a special award.

Brutus
This dachshund is a dog with no fear. He goes skydiving with his owner, Ron Sirull.

Mkombozi
A stray dog in Kenya, Mkombozi (the name, which the dog got later, means "saviour") found an abandoned human baby and kept her alive for several days until rescuers found the girl.

Reno
This police dog in Des Moines, Iowa, won an award for helping save two fellow officers, even after he was wounded by a criminal suspect.

Tommy
When his owner fell and could not get up, this dog used speed-dial on a phone to call 911 and get help.

Ueno
This faithful Akita dog continued to go to a train station daily to meet his owner – for 10 years after the owner died! A statue in Japan honours this loyal pooch.

Twiggy
A squirrel who waterskis. Seriously!

Animal Recovery

To protect animals from becoming extinct, the Committee on the Status of Endangered Wildlife in Canada (COSEWIC) looks at animal populations and basically counts them. Once we know how a species is doing, we can work to help it. They give the species a rating — from worst to best, the ratings are: Extinct, Extirpated, Endangered, Threatened, Special Concern, or Not at Risk. The good news is that, with the help of humans, some animals are taken off the list after they are no longer at risk. Here are some animals that are well along the comeback trail.

ANIMAL	PUT ON LIST	TAKEN OFF LIST
American white pelican	1978	1987
Baird's sparrow	1989	1996
Caspian swan	1978	1999
Cooper's hawk	1983	1996
Eastern bluebird	1984	1996
Gaspé shrew	1988	2006
Great grey owl	1979	1996
Humpback whale	1982	2003
Plains pocket gopher	1979	1998
Prairie long-tailed weasel	1982	1993
Prairie warbler	1985	1999
Red-shouldered hawk	1983	2006
Trumpeter swan	1978	1996

Dolphin OR Porpoise?

A marine mammal swims up to you and you want to say hi. But you don't want to embarrass yourself and it by calling it a dolphin if it's a porpoise, or a porpoise if it's a dolphin. So how do you tell the difference? Well, we're here to help with this handy clip-and-save (but not if it's a library book!) chart about these two related but different aquatic creatures. Why does this matter? Well, it would matter more if you were a dolphin or a porpoise, right?

Dolphin	Porpoise
Smaller head	Bigger head
Longer snout	Shorter snout
Larger bodies	(Usually) smaller bodies
Cone-shaped teeth	Flat, triangular teeth
Dorsal (back) fin can be curved on one edge	Fins are triangular

Bonus Confusion!

As if that wasn't confusing enough, there is a fish that goes by many names, one of which is — get this — "dolphin fish!" Its other names include dorado and mahi-mahi. So if you see "dolphin" on the menu at a seafood restaurant, it's this fish, not the friendly mammal of the same name.

The Dish on Fish

Tropical fish swimming around a pleasant aquarium can be a beautiful and calming addition to any home or classroom. There are literally hundreds of types of fish — saltwater and freshwater — that people keep as pets. Here is a list of some of the most popular (note that there are dozens of different types of some of these species).

FRESHWATER FISH

Angelfish

Betta

Cichlid

Discus

Goldfish

Gourami

Guppy

Loach

Oscar

Tetra

SALTWATER FISH

Angelfish

Clown fish

Goby

Lionfish

Wrasse

Yellow tang

Animals
Game Page

You've heard of the "circle of life," right? Where big animals eat small animals, then the big animals die and become part of the ground, and the plants grow in the ground, and the little animals eat the plants, then the big animals come along and do it all over again? Well, we've got our own little circle of life here. Starting with the number 1 and moving clockwise, fill in the blanks. The first letter of each word will be the last letter of the word in front of it. Take the letters in the shaded circles and unscramble them to find the mystery words at the bottom. Hint: They describe very familiar animals that you see all over the place!

1. Has horns and starts letters.
2. Short for really big horned African animal.
3. Big bird.
4. Boring pet in a shell (two words).
5. Don't be buffaloed!
6. A pointy whale.
7. He (or she) lives an experimental life (two words).
8. Freshwater fish.
9. Every spider is one.

_ U _ _ _   _ _ _ _ G _

CHAPTER EIGHT

Food

While reading this chapter, feel free to wipe your mouth on your sleeve, read with your elbows on the table, and eat with your hands. Just don't get food on the book! *Bon appétit!*

MORE Gross Stuff

In the first edition of the *Scholastic Canada Book of Lists*, we learned that people eat a heck of a lot of strange stuff. Sheep eyeballs in India, tarantula kebabs in Cambodia, toasted termites in South Africa, and many other unappetizing foods. Well, we didn't want to stop there. We scoured the world and found more really gross things that people actually eat. Put on a napkin (or get a bucket handy) and dig in to this list.

FOOD	WHERE THEY EAT IT
Alligator-on-a-stick	United States
Bats	Indonesia
Camel's feet	France
Cow's blood	Africa

Some cattle-herding tribes drink it straight from the cow.

Cow brain tacos	Mexico
Fish head soup	China
Fugu	Japan

A type of blowfish; if not prepared just right, it is very poisonous!

Fish eyes	Asia
Haggis	Scotland

It's the stomach of a sheep, stuffed with all the rest of its organs and roasted with oats and herbs.

Jellied eels	England

People Really Eat

Prairie oysters
Canada

Salamanders
Japan

Squirrel brains
United States

Surströmming
Sweden

It's a herring dish left out for months, so that it ends up being really, really stinky.

Turducken
United States

A turkey stuffed with a duck that has been stuffed with a chicken.

Yak butter
India, Tibet

Gross Candy

Want to eat a booger? A piece of roadkill? Some earwax? Well, you can . . . and live to tell about it. That's because lots of candymakers are using your love of gross things to make candies with yucky flavours. There are jelly beans that taste like boogers and candy shaped like squashed possums. You can eat candy dispensed from the, um, wrong end of a pig, or candy designed to look like brain drippings!

Strange Soda

Bubbly, sugary, flavoured pop (or soda, depending on where you live) is one of North America's most popular drinks. Most flavours are pretty standard: cola, lemon-lime, orange, and so on. One company, Jones Soda Co. of Washington, is different. They have created a variety of soda flavours you won't find at your local fast-food place. Check out their list of very unusual soda flavours, most made specially for Thanksgiving.

Brussels sprouts soda

Cranberry soda

Fruitcake soda

Green bean casserole soda

Mashed potato soda

Pumpkin pie soda

Turkey and gravy soda

Wild herb stuffing soda

Too busy to make a big Thanksgiving dinner? The Jones Soda Company sells its Turkey Day sodas in a special pack so that you can drink your whole meal. They've also made one-time batches of ham- and fish-taco-flavoured sodas. The cool thing is that the money they make from these is used to benefit charities like Toys for Tots!

Weird Ice Cream

Chocolate. Strawberry. Mint chip. The old standby — vanilla. Those are the ice-cream flavours we're used to. The tried and true. The traditional. Booorring! On this page, we expand our ice-cream universe and feature those flavours that go beyond the everyday, outside of the normal, and into the truly and icily odd. Many of these are only sold in Japan, but some can be found by adventurous eaters in other places. Dig in!

Fish

Guacamole
(avocado)

Lobster

Minestrone

Octopus

Pickle

Praline-chili

Salmon

Sauerkraut

Sea slug

Shrimp

Sweet potato

Whale

Poisonous Ice Cream?

One of the world leaders in bizarre ice-cream flavours is Japanese ice-cream maven Yoshiaki Sato. His shop — called Fugetsudo in Ishinomaki, Japan — has made more than 80 unusual flavours. One of the hardest to make was pit viper. Mr. Sato had to put the poisonous (but skinned and steamed) snake in a blender (yuck!), then mush it together with ice-cream fixings like sugar and cream. Small towns in Japan hire him to make fish flavours for local fairs and parties.

Champion Eaters

Don't read this list if you're hungry . . . or if you've just finished a big meal. Seriously. This list celebrates world-champion eaters, people who can shovel away an enormous amount of food in a pretty short amount of time. This "hobby" has gotten so popular that the International Federation of Competitive Eating was formed to help keep track of all the kilograms, litres, and centimetres of food going down. Looking over their long list of records, here are some of the most amazing. Oh, and please . . . don't try these at home (or school!).

FOOD	TIME	EATER	AMOUNT
Baked beans	1:48	Don Leman	2.72 kg (6 lb.)
Chicken nuggets	5:00	Sonya Thomas	80 nuggets
Chili	10:00	Richard LeFevre	5.68 l (1.5 gal.)
Cow brains	15:00	Takeru Kobayashi	8.03 kg (17.7 lb.)
Donuts	8:00	Eric Booker	49 donuts
French fries	6:00	Cookie Jarvis	2.02 kg (4.46 lb.)
Hot dogs (with buns)	12:00	Joey Chestnut	66 hot dogs
Mayonnaise	8:00	Oleg Zhornitskiy	3.78 l (128 oz.)
Onions	1:00	Eric Booker	3 @ 241 g (8.5 oz.) ea.
Pizza	10:00	Joey Chestnut	45 slices
Quesadillas	5:00	Sonya Thomas	31.4 10-cm (4-in.) quesadillas

? Takeru Kobayashi is perhaps the world's most famous speed-eater. He won the Nathan's Famous Hot Dog Eating Contest for six years running. What's amazing about him is that he's very normal-sized; he weighs only 72 kg (160 lb.). One of his competitors in 2006 weighed 193 kg (425 lb.)! Kobayashi lost out to Chestnut in 2007.

Sushi Names

Sushi is a Japanese food made of balls of flavoured rice with different toppings. Specially trained chefs put together an amazing assortment of fish, shellfish, and seaweed with rice and other ingredients. The results are colourful and tasty . . . but often raw! That's right, many types of sushi are raw fish. Don't be chicken . . . try some raw fish. Here are some of the words you'll see on sushi menus.

SUSHI	WHAT IS IT?
Nigiri sushi	Bite-sized portions of rice topped with different kinds of raw or cooked fish.
Gunkan sushi	A sort of cup made of dried seaweed and filled with rice and fish.
Maki sushi	Larger pieces of dried seaweed are covered with rice, fish, and vegetables, and then rolled. The roll is then cut into pieces. The California roll, which contains crab, avocado, and cucumber, is very popular in Canada.

Sushi ingredients

Anago	**Eel**
Ebi	**Shrimp**
Hamachi	**Yellowtail** (a kind of tuna)
Ikura	**Salmon roe**
Maguro	**Tuna**
Uni	**Sea urchin eggs**
Wasabi	**A super-hot Japanese horseradish**

Edible Flowers

Roses are pretty, but are they tasty? Nasturtiums spread their vines everywhere; what would they taste like spreading around in your mouth? You eats lots of fruits and vegetables (don't you?), so why not flowers? Here is a list of some of the many flowers that are usually safe to eat. However, before you jump into your neighbour's garden with a knife and fork, ask your parents. Flowers for eating should not have been sprayed with any pesticides or chemicals.

Bachelor's button
(petals only)

Chamomile
(also makes a lovely tea)

Chrysanthemum

Dandelion

Elderberry

Geranium

Hibiscus

Honeysuckle

Lavender

Lilac

Marigold

Mint

Nasturtium

Snapdragon

Violet
(can be candy-coated!)

? Um, "bachelor's buttons?" The puffy, often blue flowers resemble, apparently, a type of collar button or cuff link that men used to wear.

Edible Insects

Of course, *edible* (meaning something that can be eaten) and *insects* are not two words you usually expect to go together. Disgusting insects, maybe, nasty insects . . . but *edible*? Well, surprise! Insects are eaten all over the world, as snacks, main dishes, condiments, and desserts. One survey we found counted more than 1,400 types of insects that can be eaten. The good news is that most insects are very low in fat. Here are a few of the more popular types of edible (for someone else!) insects.

INSECT/HOW THEY ARE PREPARED

Ants/Fried, chocolate-covered

Ant eggs/Raw

Cockroaches/Fried, steamed

Crickets/Fried

Silkworm grubs/Steamed, fried

Caterpillars/Raw, fried

Grasshoppers/ Fried, steamed

Mealworms/ Fried, sautéed

Hu-hu grubs/Raw

Scorpion/Fried, boiled

Tarantulas/Fried

Termites/Fried

Water bugs/ Steamed, boiled

Witchetty grubs/ Various

Famous Feasts

Huge feasts have been held throughout history, to celebrate a big event or just to show off how much food a king has. Other dining events are just, well, weird. As you get ready to eat . . . er, read this list of famous feasts, tuck in your napkin, pick up your fork, and dig in.

Fit for a King (or 50)

In her very cool book *Charlemagne's Feast*, author Nichola Fletcher lists the "41,833 items of meat and poultry," including rabbits, pigs, oxen, deer, and 18 different kinds of birds, served at a 1465 feast to celebrate a new bishop in York, England.

A Mess of Mayors

In 1900, 22,295 mayors from French towns ate together on tables that were so big that some of the 3,600 waiters used bikes. The mayors downed 6,803 kg (15,000 lb.) of pheasant, salmon, and other fowl, accompanied by 50,000 bottles of wine.

Wonder What the Horses Ate

In 1903, millionaire horseman C.K. Billings hosted a dinner for 30 of his pals, but the hook was that they had to eat on horseback. Billings rented and renovated a ballroom to fit all the mounts and their eating riders.

Diamond Dining

Railroad tycoon "Diamond" Jim Brady was one of history's great eaters. Legend has it that his typical meal included three dozen oysters, six lobsters, a steak, two ducks, piles of vegetables, and soup. He didn't drink wine, so he glugged a gallon or so of orange juice. In 1905, he gave an enormous banquet honouring his racehorse.

A Bridge to Indigestion

The *Guinness World Records* book lists the world's longest table, a 5.05-km (3-mile) table set up in 1998 across a bridge in Portugal. Fifteen thousand people sat down to eat at once.

Meals in Space

How do you eat when you're flying through space? Well, pizza delivery is out, of course (though space pizza delivery person would be a cool job). And with those bulky spacesuit gloves, it's hard to hold a sandwich. Plus, that whole zero-gravity thing means that food is floating around. The folks who send the space shuttles into orbit have figured out how to let astronauts eat well and stay healthy even in zero gravity. Here is a list of space food facts.

★ Each astronaut gets three meals a day, plus some snacks.

★ The space shuttle pantry can carry as many as 70 different food items and 20 beverages.

★ Drinks include coffee, tea, orange juice, and lemonade.

★ Drinks are packaged in pouches similar to juice boxes (so the liquids won't float away).

★ Some of the food choices include macaroni and cheese, spaghetti, chicken, beef, and lots of different kinds of fish.

★ What about salt and pepper? They have it, but it's in liquid form. You can imagine what a puff of pepper floating around could do to astronauts' eyes and noses!

★ There are no refrigerators on the space shuttle, so the food is often freeze-dried; that is, the water is removed from it. To eat something like mac and cheese, the astronaut adds some water to the pouch, heats it (they do have an oven), and digs in. Well, puts a straw in, anyway.

★ What about the leftovers? Astronauts work hard, so they always clean their plates, er, pouches. All the trash is compacted and carried back to Earth for disposal. No littering in space!

Eating IN THE Armed Forces

Soldiers in the field can't stop off for fast food, and they might be kilometres away from their base when it's time to eat. That's why the well-prepared military person never leaves home without an IMP. That stands for Individual Meal Pack. Each meal pack contains an entree, a dessert, several types of beverages, a hard candy, and a package of cookies or a chocolate bar. The packs are compact and lightweight and can be heated in boiling water, or eaten cold. Here are some of the available IMP meal options — does the list make you hungry? Well, with a shelf life of three years, they may not be quite as good as a home-cooked meal . . .

IMP Breakfasts
Ham steak with mustard sauce
Omelette with salsa
Beans with wieners in tomato sauce
Scalloped potatoes and ham
Sausage and hash browns
Sausage links

IMP Lunches
Hungarian goulash
Pork with herbs and wine sauce
Macaroni with cheese sauce
Turkey and vegetable stew
Beef ravioli
Beef chop suey

IMP Dinners
Navarin (a lamb casserole)
Tarragon chicken
Chicken breast cacciatore
Cabbage rolls and tomato sauce
Salisbury steak dinner
Cheese tortellini in marinara sauce

Good with Peanut Butter

Thanks to George Washington Carver, millions of kids don't go hungry at lunch. That's because the inventive peanut expert helped perfect that smooth or chunky stuff that we just couldn't live without. (Peanut butter was first sold at the St. Louis World's Fair in 1904 by cereal maker John Kellogg.) But peanut butter, as good as it is, is usually served with something else. Whether you put it on bread, crackers, bagels, apples, or celery, here are some of the most popular or unusual food items put together with P.B. (There's actually an entire store in New York City that sells almost nothing but peanut butter–based foods.)

Bacon	Jam
Bananas	Jelly
Butter	Margarine
Chocolate	Marmalade
Fried chicken	Marshmallows
Honey	Mayonnaise

Sandwich of "The King"

Elvis Presley was one of the most famous rock singers of all time and remains a legend to his fans. Almost as famous as his music was his odd taste in food. One item he enjoyed was a fried peanut butter and banana sandwich. Make sure and use white bread to get the full "King" treatment.

Food Firsts

The first meal of the day is breakfast. That's an easy one. Here are some other food firsts you can impress your friends with.

First Candy Canes

Sugar sticks bent into cane shapes were first seen in Germany in 1670; they were all white for many years before the familiar red stripe was added.

First Sandwich

John Montagu, the Earl of Sandwich in England, didn't want to leave his card game one day in 1762. He asked for meat and cheese between slices of bread — and the sandwich was born.

First Chewing Gum

In 1848, John Curtis invented State of Maine Pure Spruce Gum.

First Potato Chips

Oh, happy day! One evening in 1853 in Saratoga Springs, New York, chef George Crum was trying to please a picky eater. He tossed some thin slices of potato in boiling oil and ta-dah! The potato chip was born.

First Coca-Cola

The world's favourite pop was first made in 1886 by John Pemberton of Atlanta, Georgia.

First Girl Guide Cookies

Those tasty treats first went on sale in 1927.

First Popsicle

Frank Epperson accidentally left a glass of lemonade outdoors one night. It was frozen the next morning, and he realized he'd discovered something cool . . . literally! First sold as the Epsicle, it became the Popsicle in 1924.

First Drive-Through Restaurant

Leading to many happy future carpool stops, this pioneering eatery opened in Glendale, California, in 1926.

First Microwave Oven

This important kitchen tool isn't food, of course, but it changed the way we make food. The first microwave oven* was sold by the Raytheon Company in 1947. It was as big as a refrigerator!

First Big Mac

McDonalds' most popular sandwich was first sold in 1968.

*Microwave ovens were actually discovered by accident when a scientist, Dr. Percy Spencer, was testing a magnetron tube and found that a chocolate bar in his pocket had melted!

Most kids would put pizza on their list of favourite foods. But kids in America's early years somehow managed to live without this essential food. The first pizzeria didn't open in North America until 1895; it was Lombardi's in New York City.

Canada's Food Guide

Eating the right foods, and the right amount of food, is an important part of growing up strong, healthy, and happy. Health Canada, the government department responsible for public health, puts out "Canada's Food Guide" to tell you how to eat well. When you make your school lunch tomorrow, try and see how well you do. These are the recommended servings in each food group for children ages 9–13.

Fruits and Vegetables

6 servings per day

EXAMPLES OF ONE SERVING: ½ cup of orange juice, 1 small apple, 1 cup of salad, 1 medium carrot

Grain Products

6 servings per day

EXAMPLES OF ONE SERVING: ½ a bagel or pita, 1 slice of bread, ½ cup cooked macaroni or rice, ¾ cup oatmeal

Milk and Alternatives

3–4 servings per day

EXAMPLES OF ONE SERVING: ¾ cup of yogourt, 50 g of cheddar cheese, 1 cup of milk

Meat and Alternatives

1–2 servings per day

EXAMPLES OF ONE SERVING: 2 eggs, 2 tablespoons of peanut butter, ¼ cup of tofu, 75 g of cold cuts

Food Chemicals

Have you ever tried to read the list of ingredients on the packaging of your favourite food? The words can be long and hard to pronounce; what do they mean? Using this list will help you understand what you are eating. By the way, ingredients on a package are listed with the highest amount named first. So, if the first ingredient is fructose, your food item has lots of sugar in it!

THE FOOD:	YOU READ ON THE LABEL:	YOU'RE EATING:
candy, cookies, cakes, beverages, fruit snacks	corn syrup, fructose, glucose, sucrose, high fructose corn syrup	sugars: sweetens the food
candy, cheese, jelly, margarine, snack foods	annatto extract, beta-carotene, caramel colour, carmine, cochineal extract, saffron	dyes: colours the food
beverages, cold cuts, cereal, snack foods	ascorbic acid, BHA, BHT, calcium propionate, calcium nitrite, citric acid, potassium sorbate	preservatives: keeps food from spoiling
candy, cake, desserts, salad dressings, snack foods	carrageenan, cellulose gel, guar gum, modified food starch, whey protein concentrate	fat replacements: lowers fat content in food
cake, jelly, desserts, salad dressings, pudding	carrageenan, gelatin, guar gum, whey, xanthan gum	thickeners: gives food specific textures
carbonated beverages, whipped cream	carbon dioxide, nitrous oxide	propellants: adds carbonation, aerates the food
bread, cereal, beverages, breakfast bars, flour	alpha tocopherols, amino acids, beta-carotene, iron sulfate, riboflavin, thiamine hydrochloride	vitamins/minerals: added back into food
bread, cakes, cookies	baking soda, calcium carbonate, monocalcium phosphate	leavening: helps food rise during baking

Famous Chefs

The most famous chef in your life, of course, is whoever in your house cooks the meals. But there are professional chefs out there who have become world famous for their way with food (and often, for their way-out personalities). Here's a short list of some of the most well-known names in the food biz.

Mario Batali New York-based chef who stars in several TV cooking shows.

Julia Child The late author and TV host made French cooking popular in America.

Bobby Flay Restaurant owner who became popular TV chef and cookbook author.

Emeril Lagasse Based in New Orleans, this TV chef is famous for saying "Bam!" when spicing food.

Nobu Matsuhisa He blends Japanese-style cooking with flavours of other nations.

Jamie Oliver His popular TV show was called *The Naked Chef*, but he wears clothes.

Wolfgang Puck A favourite of many movie stars, he turned pizza into a gourmet food.

Michael Smith A popular host of a show on Food Network Canada.

OCEAN FOOD THAT
Isn't Fish

You know all about tuna, but believe it or not, people eat other kinds of fish, too. There's more than one fish in the sea, as the old saying goes, and there's more than just fish, too. The ocean is home to hundreds of types of creatures who, through no fault of their own, are part of the world's diet. Here's a list of some animals from the sea that people enjoy eating.

Abalone	Oyster
Clam	Scallop
Conch	Sea cucumber
Crab	Shrimp
Lobster	Snail
Mussel	Squid
Octopus	

Another Kind of Chowder

You may have heard of clam chowder, but what about conch chowder? It's pronounced KONK, and is a popular dish in the Florida Keys and on Caribbean islands. In 1982, the city of Key West, Florida, declared itself an independent country (they were mostly joking) and renamed itself the Conch Republic.

Talking Food

Coming up with a list of food-related words was a piece of cake! We don't list them all here, of course, just the cream of the crop. These phrases have entered the English language hot out of the oven, ready to dress up sentences as well as dinner tables. If your favourite isn't in here, don't cry over spilled milk. You're still the apple of our eye.

apple of his/her eye
A person who is very much loved by another person

big cheese
The boss, an important person

bring home the bacon
Earn a living, support a household

butter up
Flatter or kiss up to someone

cool as a cucumber
Describing a person who is calm and confident in a tough situation

couch potato
A lazy person who watches too much TV — let's hope this isn't you!

don't cry over spilled milk
Don't make a fuss over small things or things you can't fix

egg on your face
Being embarrassed

half-baked
An idea that is incomplete or unworkable

hot dog!
An expression of enthusiasm or pleasure

in a nutshell
Describing a complicated situation in a few words

out of the frying pan and into the fire
Moving from a bad situation to one that is worse

piece of cake
Something that is easy to do

souped up
Made more fancy, improved in a cool way

spill the beans
Tell a secret

take it with a grain of salt
Expect that the information you've been given might not be true or complete

Eating
Through the Ages

Believe it or not, the ancient Egyptians and Greeks did not have fast food! That's right, they never experienced the joy of a burger served from a window to a person sitting in a car. Of course, they didn't have cars, either. Anyway, here's a look back at how much the foods people eat have changed (or not changed) through the millennia.

Ancient Egypt (about 3,500 years ago)
People ate bread made from emmer wheat; beer made from barley; fruits such as grapes, dates, figs, and melons; vegetables such as cucumbers, lettuce, onions, and garlic. Egyptians also discovered how to make marshmallows and that licorice was tasty.

Ancient Greece (about 2,500 years ago)
People ate *maza* bread made from barley and *artos* bread made from wheat. Olives were the most popular fruit, and olive oil came with most meals. Lentil soup was popular, as were figs and eggs. Fish was popular, along with squid and shellfish, but meat from animals was usually eaten only on special occasions.

Ancient Rome (2,000 years ago)
Wheat made into bread or porridge (called *puls*) was a big part of everyone's diet. Beans were common, too. Fish was available in most places, but meat was rarely served. Wine mixed with water was usually served with meals, along with yogourt. Rich folks enjoyed rare spices brought back by Rome's conquering armies. And yes, even back then,

they ate pizza in Italy – it was a flatbread topped with vegetables or cheese. (No tomato sauce, though; that vegetable didn't come over from the Americas until about 1,500 years later.)

Europe (about 1,000 years ago)

This was a very poor time, and most folks could afford little more than barley bread and what veggies they could grow themselves. Since they ate so poorly, their teeth were bad, so any meat they got was usually turned into squishy hash.

Ancient Incas (1,000 years ago)

Potatoes and corn were the most common food; they added peppers, spices, and mint for flavor. The Incas also ate squash, tomatoes, avocados, and beans of various sorts. Grains included quinoa and amaranth. The Inca people chewed kaolin, a type of clay, when they got an upset stomach. They also preserved llama meat into what they called *charqui*, which is where we get the word *jerky*, meaning dried meat.

Mongol Dynasty (about 700 years ago)

Most of the foods these folks in Asia ate came from herd animals like cattle. They ate a lot of cheese and milk, along with the meat of the animals. A broth called *shülen* was made with meat, bones, and grains. The tasty dessert we call baklava came from this era; to make it, layers of paper-thin dough are piled up with honey, nuts, dates, and sugar.

Colonial North America (400 years ago)

Archaeological digs at Jamestown found that early colonists ate tons of fish and turtles. They also ate herons, gulls, and raccoons. As other colonies became more settled, they grew grains, such as barley and wheat. Colonies along different parts of the east coast drew on their land for meat, game, fish, and birds. Meat was a big part of most meals; not too many vegetables, so you might have liked living back then!

Food
Game Page

We've got ourselves a kitchen disaster! The chef accidentally threw tonight's entire meal into the blender. Look at the ugly jumble of letters below and see if you can find a complete dinner in there. Each letter is used only once, and you should be able to find a main course (7 letters), a vegetable (9), a side dish (two words, 6 and 8), a drink (4), and a dessert (10). There are no extra letters.

CHAPTER NINE

Grab Bag

What, you thought we could fit everything in the world into the other eight chapters? As if! Fortunately, we've got this chapter into which we can cram all the other cool stuff that didn't fit into the other eight.

Sort of like the junk drawer in your house . . .

MOST
Dangerous Jobs

In Canada, about five people a day die while they're hard at work. There can be danger in almost any job if workers aren't careful. When we think of the most dangerous jobs, we often think of firefighters, police officers, and other emergency service providers. These men and women put their lives on the line for us every day. According to one study, however, these aren't the most dangerous jobs in Canada. Here is the list of the most dangerous industries to work in.

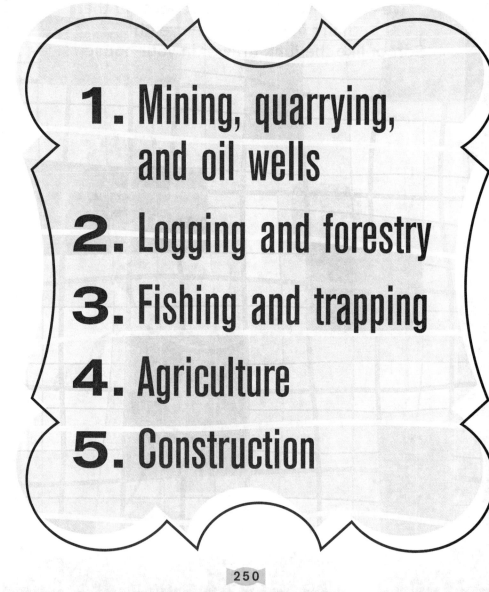

1. Mining, quarrying, and oil wells

2. Logging and forestry

3. Fishing and trapping

4. Agriculture

5. Construction

Smelliest Jobs

Lots of people think their job stinks. But these literally do!

1. Manure inspector

Yes, there are scientists who collect animal manure to study bacteria. This was named one of the worst jobs in science by *Popular Science* magazine in 2005.

2. Wastewater diver

According to the *Washington Post*, four people have this job in Mexico City. They brave stinky, rancid waters to keep the city's pumps and sewers clear.

3. Crime scene cleanup

It's a dirty, depressing job, but people in the business say the lingering smell may be the worst part.

4. Roadkill cleanup

Somebody has to remove the carcasses from the middle of the highway.

5. Portable toilet cleaner

No explanation necessary.

There's a popular TV show called *Dirty Jobs* that has featured some other really stinky ways to make a living. The host heads into the field (often in protective gear) to find out what it's like to be a sludge cleaner, a worm dung farmer, a food recycler, a skull cleaner, or even an avian vomitologist, who studies owl vomit.

What Months Are Named For

January is the gateway to a new year — which is why the month is named for the Roman god of doors and gates. Here's how each month got its name.

MONTH	NAMED FOR
January	Janus, the Roman god of doors and gates.
February	The Roman word *februalia*, which means "purification." In this month, the Romans held their festival of purification.
March	Mars, the Roman god of war. Mars was also the protector of crops and fields, and March marks the beginning of spring.
April	The Latin word *aperire*, which means "to open" (this is the time of year that flower buds open).
May	Maia, the Roman goddess of bounty.
June	Juno, the Roman goddess of marriage.
July	The Roman emperor Julius Caesar.
August	The Roman emperor Augustus Caesar.
September	The Latin word *septem*, which means "seven." This was the seventh month of the ancient Roman year.
October	The Latin word *octem*, which means "eight." This was the eighth month of the ancient Roman year.
November	The Latin word *novem*, which means "nine." This was the ninth month of the ancient Roman year.
December	The Latin word *decem*, which means "ten." This was the tenth month of the ancient Roman year.

DAYS OF THE
Week

Sunday's origin lies in the sun, and Monday's in the moon, but the rest of the days of the week aren't so obvious. Here's how each day got its name.

DAY	NAMED FOR
Sunday	Sunne, the German goddess of the sun.
Monday	Mani, the German god of the moon.
Tuesday	Tyr (in Old English, the name was Tiu or Tew), the Norse god of war.
Wednesday	Odin (in German mythology, the name was Woden), the chief god in Norse mythology.
Thursday	Thor, the Norse god of thunder.
Friday	Freya, the Norse goddess of love and beauty.
Saturday	Saturn, the Roman god of agriculture.

Things are different in Turkmenistan. Its ruler, Saparmurat Niyazov, renamed January after his title, "Turkmenbashi," and April after his mom. Tuesday is "Young Day," Wednesday is now "Favourable Day," and Sunday is "Spirit Day."

MORE
Wild Phobias

Here's one more item we need to add to this ever-expanding list: a fear of phobias. Yes, there's a name for that, too! It's phobophobia.

Arachibutyrophobia
IS THE FEAR OF peanut butter sticking to the roof of your mouth

Blennophobia
IS THE FEAR OF slime

Defecaloesiophobia
IS THE FEAR OF painful bowel movements

Eisoptrophobia
IS THE FEAR OF seeing yourself in a mirror

Hippopotomonstrosesquippedaliophobia
IS THE FEAR OF long words

Liticaphobia
IS THE FEAR OF lawsuits

Novercaphobia
IS THE FEAR OF your stepmother

Octophobia
IS THE FEAR OF the figure 8

Paraskavedekatriaphobia
IS THE FEAR OF Friday the 13th

Pteronophobia
IS THE FEAR OF being tickled by feathers

Most Common Last Names

The list below is of the most common last names in Canada. The list was collected using phone books from across the country. Here's a chance to create your own list. Using your own local phone book, make a list of the most common last names in your city, town or municipality. How does yours compare with the nationwide list below?

1. Li
2. Smith
3. Lam
4. Martin
5. Brown
6. Roy
7. Tremblay
8. Lee
9. Gagnon
10. Wilson

11. Clark
12. Johnson
13. White
14. Williams
15. Côté
16. Taylor
17. Campbell
18. Anderson
19. Chan
20. Jones

Scouts AND Guides

Looking for some fun and adventure in the great outdoors? Many children choose to join Scouts Canada, for boys and girls, or Girl Guides, for girls only! Each group has different levels based on how old you are. See where you fit in . . . and we'll see you around the campfire!

SCOUTS CANADA

Beavers (ages 5–7)
Cubs (ages 8–10)
Scouts (ages 11–14)
Venturers (ages 14–17)
Rovers (ages 18–26)

GIRL GUIDES

Sparks (ages 5–6)
Brownies (ages 7–8)
Guides (ages 9–11)
Pathfinders (ages 12–14)
Rangers (ages 15–17)
Women (ages 18 and up)

? Who's the chief? The Chief Scout of Canada is the scout leader. Who gets to be Chief Scout? Since 1910, that title has gone to the current Governor General.

FAVOURITE
Playground Games

All you need are two or more kids, some free time, and open space to play one of the oldest and most fun playground games ever: tag. Here are some other popular favourites that have stood the test of time.

1. Capture the Flag

2. Jump Rope

3. Four Square

4. Ghost in the Graveyard

5. Handball

6. Hide and Seek

7. Hopscotch

8. Pickle (Monkey in the Middle)

9. Red Light, Green Light

10. Red Rover

Most Expensive Items
Sold on eBay

A round of golf with Tiger Woods was sold for $425,000 on the online auction site eBay. That almost seems like a bargain compared to these items.

	ITEM	PRICE
1.	340-year-old copy of Shakespeare's *Pericles, Prince of Tyre*	**$9,300,000**
2.	Grumman Gulfstream II jet	**$4,900,000**
3.	San Lorenzo 80 motor yacht	**$1,935,300**
4.	1909 Honus Wagner baseball card	**$1,265,000**
5.	Kentucky's Diamond Lake Resort	**$1,200,000**

One Amazing Place

Since it was launched in 1999, eBay has become a major part of world commerce. More used cars are sold through eBay than any other place. People use the site to sell just about anything you can think of. In 2004, someone sold a complete 50,000-year-old mammoth skeleton (named Max). More than 125 million people use the site regularly and many people have started small businesses doing nothing but buying and selling. It works pretty simply: Once you're registered (and you need a credit card!), you offer items and anyone can bid on them. At the end of the auction, the highest price gets the item; you get paid and then ship it.

What's in
Toothpaste?

We'll spare you the technical names of the ingredients, which can vary from brand to brand, but here's what is in that paste you brush your teeth with (after every meal, of course!).

Abrasives
Removes plaque and stains, and polishes teeth

Colouring agents
Turns plain toothpaste into a rainbow of colours

Detergents
Creates foaming action (or else the paste would dribble out of your mouth!)

Flavouring agents/sweeteners
Covers up the natural taste of the toothpaste (especially the yucky detergents)

Fluoride
Helps protect against cavities and strengthens tooth enamel

Humectants
Keeps toothpaste from drying out

Preservatives
Keeps toothpaste fresh and means you don't have to keep it in the fridge

Thickeners
Gives the paste texture

Barbie's Careers

From sports to politics to public service, there's almost nothing the famous (and talented!) doll hasn't tried. Here are just some of her many areas of expertise.

1. **Actress**
   (and singer and rock star, too)
2. **Army officer**
   (Air Force, Marine Corps, and Navy)
3. **Astronaut**
4. **Babysitter**
5. **Ballerina**
6. **Basketball player**
7. **Circus star**
8. **Dentist**
9. **Doctor**
10. **Fashion model**
    (and designer and photographer, too)
11. **Firefighter**
12. **Flight attendant**
13. **Lifeguard**
14. **Nurse**
15. **Olympic gymnast**
    (and figure skater)
16. **Paleontologist**
17. **Police officer**
18. **Presidential candidate**
19. **Teacher**
20. **Veterinarian**

THINGS
People Race

People have raced cars and bicycles and boats pretty much since the first time they hit the road (or the sea, depending). But folks will race just about anything, including these unusual vehicles.

1. Bathtubs
2. 18-wheel trucks
3. Golf carts
4. Kinetic sculptures
5. Lawn mowers
6. Shopping carts
7. Soapboxes
8. Toilets
9. Tractors
10. Wheelbarrows

? Toilet racing? That's right, folks have figured out how to put motors in toilets and zoom down a track. Yes, you sit on them just like you'd sit on a toilet, but no, you keep your clothes on. And you don't need paper.

Land Speed Records

Andy Green, a fighter pilot for Britain's Royal Air Force, broke the sound barrier when he set the current land speed record (the record for going the fastest on dry land) in 1997. He did it in a rocket-powered car. Here are the record holders at various selected intervals.

DATE	CAR/DRIVER	KPH/MPH
Dec. 18, 1898	Jeantaud/Gaston Chasseloup-Laubat	63.15/39.24
Jan. 17, 1899	Jenatzy/Camille Jenatzy	66.66/41.42
Mar. 4, 1899	Jeantaud/Gaston Chasseloup-Laubat	92.70/57.60
Apr. 29, 1899	Jenatzy/Camille Jenatzy	105.88/65.79
Apr. 13, 1902	Serpollet/Leon Serpollet	120.80/75.06
Jul. 17, 1903	Gobron-Brillie/Arthur Duray	134.33/83.47
Mar. 31, 1904	Gobron-Brillie/Louis Rigolly	152.53/94.78
Jul. 21, 1904	Gobron-Brillie/Louis Rigolly	166.65/103.55
Jul. 21, 1925	Sunbeam/Malcolm Campbell	242.62/150.76
Mar. 29, 1927	Sunbeam/Henry Segrave	327.97/203.79
Feb. 24, 1932	Bluebird/Malcolm Campbell	408.72/253.97
Sept. 3, 1935	Bluebird/Malcolm Campbell	484.62/301.13
Sept. 15, 1938	Railton/John Cobb	563.59/350.20
Jul. 17, 1964	Bluebird/Donald Campbell	648.73/403.10
Oct. 5, 1964	Wingfoot Express/Tom Green	698.49/434.02
Oct. 13, 1964	Spirit of America/Craig Breedlove	754.33/468.72
Oct. 15, 1964	Spirit of America/Craig Breedlove	846.97/526.28
Oct. 27, 1964	Green Monster/Art Arfons	863.75/536.71
Nov. 2, 1965	Spirit of America-Sonic I/Craig Breedlove	893.96/555.48
Nov. 7, 1965	Green Monster/Art Arfons	927.87/576.55
Nov. 15, 1965	Spirit of America-Sonic I/Craig Breedlove	966.57/600.60
Oct. 23, 1970	Blue Flame/Gary Gabelich	1,001.67/622.41
Oct. 4, 1983	Thrust 2/Richard Noble	1,019.47/633.47
Oct. 15, 1997	Thrust SSC/Andy Green	1,227.99/763.04

U.F.O. Sightings

Is there life out there in space? Here are ten of the most well-known sightings of U.F.O.s (Unidentified Flying Objects). Have you ever seen one? Or are you a space alien yourself? If so, please contact us — we've got a lot of questions to ask you!

June 1947: While piloting his plane, Kenneth Arnold spotted a formation of unidentified aircraft and unwittingly coined the term "flying saucer."

July 1947: Not long after the Kenneth Arnold incident, the remnants of what was originally reported as a crashed "flying disk" were recovered near Roswell, New Mexico.

September 1961: While vacationing in Canada, New Hampshire's Betty and Barney Hill claimed to be "spacenapped" by a U.F.O.

May 1967: Stephen Michalak, a prospector working near Falcon Lake, Manitoba, reported seeing two revolving disks. When he tried to touch one, he received a mysterious burn on his chest.

January 1969: Future president Jimmy Carter, then the governor of Georgia, spotted a U.F.O. outside the Lions Club in Leary, Georgia, where he was to give a speech.

September 1976: An Iranian Air Force pilot gave chase to an unidentified aircraft over Tehran. He could not fire a missile because his instrumentation was disabled. A second pilot had the same mechanical trouble until the U.F.O. left them behind.

December 1980: Betty Cash and two others driving through Piney Woods, Texas, saw a diamond-shaped object in the sky, soon followed by nearly two dozen military helicopters.

January 1981: French farmer Renato Nicolai spotted a small flying disk while working in his yard. It touched down, leaving behind changes in the landscape that authorities could not explain.

November 1989: A large, triangular craft quietly moved across the landscape of Belgium. Over the next several months, more than 1,000 sightings were reported.

March 1997: Numerous witnesses reported a series of unexplained lights moving in formation across the Arizona sky.

Haunted Canada

Do you believe that the ghostly cry of a logging-camp cook can haunt a museum? Or that a flaming ship whose pirate crew made a pact with the devil can mysteriously appear in a harbour? How about a dead painter who is said to stalk the hallway where his unfinished masterpiece hangs? If so, then pack up your ghost-tracking equipment, kids, 'cause it's time to go ghost hunting! Here is a list of haunted places across the country.

Banff Springs Hotel,
Banff, Alberta

Billy Bishop Legion Hall,
Vancouver, British Columbia

Empress Theatre,
Fort Macleod, Alberta

Fort Garry Hotel,
Winnipeg, Manitoba

Gibraltar Point Lighthouse,
Toronto Islands, Toronto, Ontario

Government House,
Regina, Saskatchewan

HI Ottawa Jail Hostel,
Ottawa, Ontario

Old Montreal,
Montreal, Quebec

Old Spaghetti Factory,
Gastown, Vancouver, British Columbia

Olde Angel Inn,
Niagara-on-the-Lake, Ontario

Queen's Road,
St. John's, Newfoundland

St. Louis railway tracks,
St. Louis, Saskatchewan

West Point Lighthouse,
O'Leary, Prince Edward Island

Woodsmen's Museum,
Boiestown, New Brunswick

Ghostly Presidents

Ghosts in the White House, home of U.S. presidents?
Since it was built in the early 1800s, the White House has
supposedly been home to several ghosts. Visitors, First
Families, and guests have all reported seeing such strange
sights as Abigail Adams doing her laundry; Dolly Madison
in the Rose Garden; and Abraham Lincoln in the hallways.

Fastest Cars
You Can Buy

Forbes magazine found these cars to be the fastest that you can buy. Just be prepared to spend a few hundred thousand dollars for each one!

CAR	TOP SPEED (KPH/MPH)
1. Saleen S7 Twin Turbo	418/260
2. Koenigsegg CCR	389/242
3. Koenigsegg CC8S	386/240
4. Ultima Can-Am 640 & GTR 640	372/231
5. Spyker C8 Double 12 S	346/215
6. Mercedes-Benz SLR McLaren	333/207
7. Evans 387 & 487	331/206
8. Ford GT	330/205
9. Lamborghini Murciélago	330/205
10. Porsche Carrera GT	330/205

Useful Mnemonics

A mnemonic (pronounced *ni-MON-ik*) device is a helpful way to remember things. Here are a few worth, well . . . remembering.

Spring forward, fall back.
It comes in handy twice a year for remembering which way to adjust your clocks when the time changes.

***I* before e, except after c.**
To help with your spelling. The weird thing, though, is that there are a lot of exceptions to this rule.

Red sky at night, sailor's delight; red sky at morning, sailor's take warning.
To help forecast the weather.

There's a rat in *separate*.
To remember how to spell this commonly misspelled word.

Richard of York gave battle in vain.
Use the first letter of each word to remember the colours of the rainbow: red, orange, yellow, green, blue, indigo, violet. You can also just remember the name Roy G. Biv.

Father Charles goes down and ends battle.
In music, take the first letter of each word to remember the order of the sharps: F, C, G, D, A, E, B.

Every good boy does fine.
Also in music, the ascending order of the notes in the treble clef: E, G, B, D, F.

My very eager mother served just us nuts.
The first letters are the initials, in order, of the planets. Until 2006, it ended with "nine pizzas" to include Pluto.

Going Camping

It's not just about pitching a tent and roasting marshmallows anymore. These days, kids can find a summer camp for just about anything you can imagine. Here are just a few examples.

Acting camp	Fitness camp
Cheerleading camp	Rock 'n' roll camp
Computer camp	Scuba camp
Culinary camp	Space camp
Filmmaking camp	Theatre camp

First Camps

In Canada, Camp Stephens in Ontario opened in 1891. Camps in Keewaydin, Ontario, and Kanawana, Quebec, started in 1894. Down south, the Boy Scouts of America opened Camp Owasippe in Michigan in 1910. The Girl Scouts, formed in 1912, opened their first camp at Camp Bonnie Brae, in Massachusetts, that year.

Biggest Statues

New York's Statue of Liberty may be one of the most famous statues in the world, but it's not the tallest. That distinction belongs to a Buddha statue in Japan that is two-and-a-half times taller than the Statue of Liberty. Here are some other huge statues throughout the world.

STATUE/SITE	HEIGHT (METRES/FEET)
Amida Buddha/Ushiku, Japan	**120/394**
Mother Russia Statue/Volgograd, Russia	**82.3/270**
Lishan Buddha/Sichuan Province, China	**67/220**
Statue of Liberty/New York, New York	**46/151**
Wat Pho Buddha*/Bangkok, Thailand	**46/151**
Cosmoplanetary Messiah/Castellane, France	**32.6/107**
Christ Redeemer/Rio de Janeiro, Brazil	**29.9/98**

*This one is actually lying down, not standing up!

Here's a list of some cool facts about the Statue of Liberty:
- The total weight of copper and steel in the statue is 141,500 kg (312,000 lb.).
- There are 25 windows in the crown.
- One index finger alone is 2.4 m (8 ft.).
- Liberty Island, where the statue is located, was once known as Bedloe's Island.

Knock, Knock

Here are our picks for the good and the bad in the world of knock-knock jokes. Of course, your opinion may vary!

Best

"Knock, knock."
"Who's there?"
"Interrupting cow."
"Interrupting cow–"
"Mooooooooo!"

"Knock, knock."
"Who's there?"
"Boo."
"Boo who?"
"Don't cry. It's only a knock-knock joke."

"Knock, knock."
"Who's there?"
"Nobel."
"Nobel who?"
"No bell, so I knocked!"

"Knock, knock."
"Who's there?"
"Little old lady."
"Little old lady who?"
"I didn't know you could yodel!"

"Knock, knock."
"Who's there?"
"Boyd."
"Boyd who?"
"Boy, do you ask a lot of questions!"

"Knock, knock."
"Who's there?"
"Police."
"Police who?"
"Police let us in. It's cold!"

Worst

Some knock-knock jokes are so bad that they're good. We'll let you decide if these qualify.

"Knock, knock."

"Who's there?"

"Lettuce."

"Lettuce who?"

"[sing] Let us entertain you. Let us make you smile!"

"Knock, knock."

"Who's there?"

"Who."

"Who who?"

"Uh-oh, there's an owl at the door!"

"Knock, knock."

"Who's there?"

"Toodle."

"Toodle who?"

"Good-bye!"

"Knock, knock."

"Who's there?"

"Banana."

"Banana who?"

"Knock, knock."

"Who's there?"

"Banana."

"Banana who?"

"Knock, knock."

"Who's there?"

"Orange."

"Orange who?"

"Orange you glad I didn't say banana?"

"Knock, knock."

"Who's there?"

"Atch."

"Atch who?"

"Gesundheit!"

Amazing Bodies

Rings through the tongue? Intentional scarring? These real-life body modifications will make you say, "Ewwwww!" (or "Ouch!").

✳ In Myanmar (formerly known as Burma), women in the Padaung tribe stretch their necks by wearing a series of neck rings. They consider it a sign of beauty and stature.

✳ In some cultures (in certain tribes in Ethiopia and Brazil, for instance), large plates, or plugs, are inserted into the lower lip to stretch it far beyond the usual proportions.

✳ According to *Ripley's Believe It or Not!: Planet Eccentric,* the world's most-pierced woman lives in Scotland. Elaine Davidson has close to 6,005 piercings. She can put her finger through her tongue!

✳ Cuba's Luis Antonio Aguero is reportedly the world's most-pierced man. He has 230 body piercings.

✳ Remember Mr. Spock on television's *Star Trek*? A man in China had plastic surgery to give him the same pointy ears as the universe's most famous Vulcan.

✳ Dennis Avner of Whidbey Island, Washington, is better known as Catman or Stalking Cat. He's made many body alterations — including implants to allow for whiskers — so he can resemble a tiger.

✳ The Lizard Man is Erik Sprague, a performer whose many body modifications give him the appearance of a reptile. He's even got a bifurcated tongue — that means it's forked, like a lizard's.

Grab Bag
Game Page

It's a grab bag chapter . . . so we've got a grab bag game. There are four different puzzles below, all in different formats. Complete all the puzzles and then take the letters that end up in (or are already in) the shaded circles and unscramble them to find something from this chapter that goes on your teeth. Note: All the answers to the various puzzles can be found in this chapter . . . somewhere!

1. Fill in the blank letters to find the mystery word:

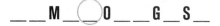

___ ___ M ___ ◯ O ___ ___ G ___ S ___

2. Unscramble these letters to find something from the chapter.

HHDTODPWAABU ___ ___ ___   ___ ___ ___   ___ ___ ___ ___ ___ ___

3. Which item doesn't belong on the list?

Spyker, Evans, Porsche, Can-Am, Conor, Ford:

_____

4. Fill in the blanks of this mini word snake. Except for the first word, the first letter of each word is the last letter of the word ahead of it.

A. Gave his name to January   C. Job of July's name origin

B. Namesake of nearest star   D. Calendar we got four months from

Mystery word:

___ ___ ___ ___ ___ ___ ___ ___

CHAPTER TEN

Sports

Banana slugs, a catch-can man, niblicks, spoons, sepak takraw, Saran Wrap, Salchows, and flying camels: What do all these have to do with sports? Read on to find out.

Greatest Athletes

A few years ago, as the 1900s turned into the 2000s, people created tons of "best-of-the-century" lists. This one is taken from a list of the best North American athletes of the 1900s, as chosen by a panel of experts brought together by ESPN. How many have you heard of? If you haven't, check 'em out . . . they were amazing.

Hank Aaron, baseball

Muhammad Ali, boxing

Wilt Chamberlain, basketball

Ty Cobb, baseball

Babe Didrikson Zaharias, track & field and golf

Wayne Gretzky, hockey

Gordie Howe, hockey

Michael Jordan, basketball

Carl Lewis, track & field

Joe Louis, boxing

of the 20th Century

Willie Mays, baseball

Martina Navratilova, tennis

Jack Nicklaus, golf

Jesse Owens, track & field

Babe Ruth, baseball

Jim Thorpe, track & field, baseball, and football

Jackie Robinson, baseball

Ted Williams, baseball

Great Canadians

The CBC held a poll in 2004 that chose the Ten Greatest Canadians (see page 59). How cool is it that three of them are sports figures: NHL star Wayne Gretzky, hockey broadcaster Don Cherry, and runner Terry Fox?

Red Dogs AND Blitzes

Every sport has its own language, but football seems to create more unique terminology than most sports. *Touchdown* and *kickoff* you know, but here's a list of some unusual slang terms that will let you fit into any huddle you join.

Blitz On this defensive play, linebackers, cornerbacks, or safeties all rush the quarterback at the snap, instead of going back in pass coverage.

Hail Mary A long pass thrown up for grabs (like a prayer), often at the end of a half or a game.

Mike, Sam, and Will These are nicknames for the middle, strongside (opposite the tight end), and weakside linebackers.

Pancake A block by an offensive player that puts a defender flat on his back.

Read Just like you're reading this book, quarterbacks and coaches have to "read" a defense, trying to see how they're going to line up for a play.

Red dog A sort of old-fashioned name for a blitz.

The Rock The football.

Snot-bubbler A hit by a defender that is so hard the player with the ball has, um, something coming out of his nose.

Take it to the house Carry the ball into the end zone for a touchdown.

Thumper A defensive player adept at producing snot-bubblers.

NFL Uniform Rules

There's an old saying in sports: "You can't tell the players without a scorecard." Well, in the NFL that's only partly true. In 1973, the league put in place a numbering system, assigning numbers to each position group. The latest change to the system came in 2004, when the league added receivers to the 10–19 group.

NUMBERS	POSITIONS
1–9	Quarterbacks and kickers
10–19	Quarterbacks, receivers, and kickers
20–49	Running backs and defensive backs
50–59	Centres and linebackers
60–79	Defensive linemen and offensive linemen
80–89	Receivers and tight ends
90–99	Defensive linemen and linebackers

! A tiny handful of players over the years have worn numbers that are not on this list. The most famous of them was the Raiders' Hall-of-Fame centre Jim Otto, who wore, as his double-O name suggests, 00. Houston receiver Ken Burrough wore 00. Running back John Olsewski was the only NFL No. 0 we could find.

NBA Big & Small

Being tall is usually important for NBA players, so here's a list of the tallest of the tall, the most sky-high players in NBA history. But short players can succeed, too, with quickness and great ball-handling skills. So we've also got a list of the shortest players in league history. It just goes to show, it's not the size of the athlete, it's the size of his heart that counts — but being tall does help!

TALLEST

HEIGHT (CM/FT. IN.)	PLAYER
231/7 ft. 7 in.	Manute Bol
	Gheorghe Muresan
228/7 ft. 6 in.	Shawn Bradley
226/7 ft. 5 in.	Chuck Nevitt
	Slavko Vranes
	Yao Ming
193/7 ft. 4 in.	Mark Eaton
	Priest Lauderdale
	Ralph Sampson
	Rik Smits

SHORTEST

160/5 ft. 3 in.	Muggsy Bogues
165/5 ft. 5 in.	Earl Boykins
170/5 ft. 7 in.	Jerry Dover
	Greg Grant
	Keith Jennings
	Herm Klotz
	Vat Misaka
	Monte Towe
	Spud Webb

Famous Dunks

The slam dunk is basketball's most popular play. Players seem to defy gravity as they soar through the air. Toss in some midair gymnastics and the power of the final slam into the basket, and you've got one crowd-pleasing manoeuvre. Here is a list of some of the most famous or important dunks in basketball history.

Jason Richardson, 2003

Voted by fans as the best-ever in the NBA's annual dunk contest, Richardson leaped, passed the ball between his legs, and then reached back behind his head to slam the ball home.

Lisa Leslie, 2002

The Los Angeles Sparks star made the first slam dunk in the history of the WNBA.

Vince Carter, 2000

At the Olympics, Carter leapfrogged over a 218 cm (7 ft. 2 in.) French player to dunk the ball.

Michael Jordan, 1991

So good he's on here twice: Jordan's dunk over Patrick Ewing in the playoffs was the number-one dunk on the 1999 DVD "NBA's 100 Greatest Plays."

Michael Jordan, 1988

During the NBA slam-dunk contest, "Air" Jordan leaped all the way from the free-throw line to the basket to slam it home!

Spud Webb, 1986

Though only 170 cm (5 ft. 7 in.), Spud had major hops. He won the slam-dunk contest with a 360-degree-spin slam.

Lorenzo Charles, 1983

This wasn't the prettiest, but perhaps the most important. Charles caught a missed shot and slammed it home as time expired to give North Carolina State an upset NCAA championship over Houston.

Julius "Dr. J" Erving, 1983

This early dunkmaster's 1983 slam over Kareem Abdul-Jabbar of the Lakers is an all-time great.

Baseball
by the Numbers

Baseball is a game simply chock full of numbers. There are statistics for just about anything. If you want to know a player's average while batting left-handed on Tuesdays in May against right-handers in a domed stadium, you can find that out. But most of those numbers disappear quickly. Others stand the test of time and are as recognizable to longtime fans as the names of the players themselves. Here are a handful of baseball's most famous statistics.

NUMBER	MEANING
3	Uniform number of the great Babe Ruth
24	Uniform number of all-around star Willie Mays
56	Record number of consecutive games with a hit by Joe DiMaggio in 1941
61	Single-season home run total by Roger Maris in 1961, the record until Mark McGwire broke it in 1998
73	Current single-season homer mark, set by Barry Bonds in 2003
191	Single-season RBI record set by Hack Wilson in 1930
.366	All-time best career batting average of Ty Cobb
.406	1941 batting average of Ted Williams, the last man to hit above .400
511	Career-record pitching wins by Cy Young
755	Home run total of Hank Aaron, second-most ever
2,130	Consecutive-games-played streak by Lou Gehrig, 1923–1939*
4,191**	Ty Cobb's career hits total, the record until Pete Rose broke it in 1985

*Gehrig held the record until 1995, when Cal Ripken, Jr. broke it. But Ripken's final total of 2,632 hasn't really gained the same fame . . . yet.

**Research in the 1990s found that this number, famous for decades, was wrong; Cobb's career total is now listed as 4,189. However, the 4,191 number is still much more well-known.

Perfect Games

In baseball, a perfect game is one in which a pitcher wins the game while retiring every single batter he faces. That is, not one opposing batter reaches base in any way: hit, error, walk, or whatever. In pro baseball's nearly 150-year history, there have been only 17 perfect games pitched (through 2008). Don Larsen's is the only one to have been pitched in the World Series.

PITCHER, TEAM	YEAR
J. Lee Richmond, Brown Stockings	1880
J. Montgomery Ward, Grays	1880
Cy Young, Red Sox	1904
Addie Joss, Indians	1908
Charley Robertson, Tigers	1922
Don Larsen, Yankees	1956
Jim Bunning, Phillies	1964
Jim "Catfish" Hunter, Athletics	1968
Len Barker, Indians	1981
Mike Witt, Angels	1984
Tom Browning, Reds	1988
Dennis Martinez, Expos	1991
Kenny Rogers, Rangers	1994
David Wells, Yankees	1998
David Cone, Yankees	1999
Randy Johnson, Diamondbacks	2004

Super Sluggers

Homer, tater, dinger, long ball, goin' yard, big fly, "Goodbye, Mr. Spalding" — whatever you call it (and there are dozens more nicknames), the home run is baseball's greatest hit. The players on this list of the all-time career home run leaders* are among baseball's most famous and celebrated players. Going, going . . . gone!

PLAYER, TEAM	HOMERS*
Barry Bonds**	762
Hank Aaron	755
Babe Ruth	714
Willie Mays	660
Ken Griffey, Jr.**	611
Sammy Sosa	609
Frank Robinson	586
Mark McGwire	583
Harmon Killebrew	573
Rafael Palmeiro	569
Reggie Jackson	563
Alex Rodriguez**	553
Mike Schmidt	548
Jim Thome**	541
Mickey Mantle	536

*Statistics through 2008 season. **Active through 2008.

CFL Records

Some of the teams in the Canadian Football League have been kicking, running, and passing since the 1860s. The CFL itself was officially founded in 1958. Here are some of the most famous career records in CFL history.

Most rushing yards
Mike Pringle, 16,425

Most touchdowns
Milt Stegall, 144

Most passing yards
72,381, Damon Allen

Most touchdown passes
394, Damon Allen

Most receptions
1,006, Terry Vaughn

Most receiving yards
Allen Pitts, 14,891

Most touchdown catches
Milt Stegall, 141

Most points scored
Lui Passasglia, 3,991

Most interceptions
Less Browne, 87

Who's Who in the
Pit Crew

Did you ever notice that whenever they interview a NASCAR driver after the race, he always says "we?" He'll say, "We had a great race." Or "We drove well today." Who is he talking about? Was there someone else in the car with him? How many steering wheels does his car have, anyway? Well, of course, he's not talking about people in the car with him; he's all alone in there out on the track. He's talking about the important support team behind him: the pit crew. When he stops during a race, these highly trained experts leap into action. They can change four tires and fill up the gas tank in about 18 seconds! Each NASCAR pit crew has seven main members; here is a list of their jobs and responsibilities.

The Jack Man

He carries a long-handled floor jack. With one pump of the handle, he lifts one side of the car off the ground. After the tires are changed on that side, he lowers the car and sprints around to the other side. When the second pair of tires is changed, he checks his crew, drops the car, and signals the driver to take off.

Tire Carriers

One each for the front and rear – they lug new 36-kg (80-lb.) tires over the wall separating the crew area from the track. After the old tires are removed, they quickly carry them back over the wall. The job demands balance and strength.

Tire Changers

Using an air gun, these two crew members – again, one each for the front and rear tires – remove the lug nuts that attach the tire to the car (they can unscrew five in about two seconds!), then hang a new tire and screw the nuts back on. Then they race around to the other side of the car and repeat the process.

Gas Can Man

At the rear of the car, this crew member empties two 41.6-l (11-gallon) containers of gasoline into the tank. He wears a special protective face mask because of fuel fumes, plus a fireproof apron.

Catch-Can Man

The gas can man's assistant hands him the full cans and takes away the empties. He helps catch any overflow fuel to prevent fires. He also stands ready to assist any other crew member who needs help.

Off the Track

A NASCAR team also includes:

• A crew chief, who supervises the entire team and communicates with the driver during the race

• Spotters, who sit high above the track and radio in reports from around the track

• Crew assistants, who use long poles to deliver water to the driver, clean the windshield, and clean debris off the front air grille

NASCAR's Tracks

NASCAR holds 36 races each season at tracks around the United States. The schedule changes slightly from year to year, but these tracks are almost always on the annual roster. Some of these tracks are the site of two or more races per season.

TRACK NAME	LOCATION
Atlanta Motor Speedway	Atlanta, Georgia
Bristol Motor Speedway	Bristol, Tennessee
California Speedway	Fontana, California
Chicagoland Speedway	Joliet, Illinois
Darlington Raceway	Darlington, South Carolina
Daytona International Speedway	Daytona Beach, Florida
Dover International Speedway	Dover, Delaware
Homestead-Miami Speedway	Homestead, Florida
Indianapolis Speedway	Indianapolis, Indiana
Infineon Raceway	Sonoma, California
Kansas Speedway	Kansas City, Kansas
Las Vegas Motor Speedway	Las Vegas, Nevada
Lowe's Motor Speedway	Charlotte, North Carolina
Martinsville Speedway	Martinsville, Virginia
Michigan International Speedway	Brooklyn, Michigan
New Hampshire International Speedway	Loudon, New Hampshire
Talladega Superspeedway	Talladega, Alabama
Texas Motor Speedway	Justin, Texas
Phoenix International Raceway	Phoenix, Arizona
Pocono Raceway	Long Pond, Pennsylvania
Richmond International Raceway	Richmond, Virginia
Watkins Glen International	Watkins Glen, New York

NASCAR's
Families

Since its beginnings in 1948, NASCAR has always included many families among its driving teams. Fathers and sons, brothers, cousins, even sisters have all taken part in NASCAR races. In fact, one family, the Frances, has owned NASCAR since its founding. This list includes just a few of the more prominent NASCAR families (listed from oldest to youngest members).

Bodine
Geoffrey, Brett, Todd

Earnhardt
Ralph, Dale Sr.*, Dale Jr., Kerry

Flock
Tim*, Fonty, Bob, Ethel

Jarrett
Ned*, Dale*

Labonte
Terry*, Bobby*

Petty
Lee*, Richard*, Kyle, Adam

Wallace
Rusty*, Mike, Kenny

Waltrip
Darrell*, Michael

*Won at least one NASCAR season championship

Hockey Heroes

The National Hockey League has some of the coolest-looking and most famous postseason awards in sports. They don't just put out an MVP, they choose winners in several categories. The trophies call to mind the greatest names in the game. Here are some facts and stats about all of the NHL's major awards.

Hart Memorial
GIVEN TO: **most valuable player**
NAMED FOR: **David Hart, donor of original trophy**
2007–2008 WINNER: **Alex Ovechkin, Washington**
MOST WINS: **9, Wayne Gretzky**

Lester B. Pearson Award
GIVEN TO: **NHL Players' Association most valuable player**
NAMED FOR: **former Canadian prime minister**
2007–2008 WINNER: **Alex Ovechkin, Washington**
MOST WINS: **5, Wayne Gretzky**

Norris Memorial
GIVEN TO: **top defenseman**
NAMED FOR: **James Norris, former owner of Red Wings**
2007–2008 WINNER: **Nicklas Lidstrom, Detroit**
MOST WINS: **8, Bobby Orr**

Calder Memorial
GIVEN TO: **top rookie**
NAMED FOR: **Frank Calder, former NHL president**
2007–2008 WINNER: **Patrick Kane, Chicago**
MOST WINS: **can only be won once!**

Vezina Trophy
GIVEN TO: **most outstanding goalkeeper**
NAMED FOR: **Canadiens goalie Georges Vezina, who died in 1925**
2007–2008 WINNER: **Martin Brodeur, New Jersey**
MOST WINS: **7, Jacques Plante**

Lady Byng Memorial
GIVEN TO: **most gentlemanly player**
NAMED FOR: **wife of Canada's governor general in 1925**
2007–2008 WINNER: **Pavel Datsyuk, Detroit**
MOST WINS: **7, Frank Boucher**

Art Ross Trophy
GIVEN TO: **top scorer**
NAMED FOR: **Arthur Ross, former Boston Bruins coach**
2007–2008 WINNER: **Alex Ovechkin, Washington**
MOST WINS: **9, Wayne Gretzky**

Frank J. Selke Trophy
GIVEN TO: **most outstanding defensive forward**
NAMED FOR: **longtime Canadiens coach and general manager**
2007–2008 WINNER: **Pavel Datsyuk, Detroit**
MOST WINS: **4, Bob Gainey**

Jack Adams Award
GIVEN TO: **top coach**
NAMED FOR: **longtime Red Wings coach**
2007–2008 WINNER: **Bruce Boudreau, Washington**
MOST WINS: **several coaches with two**

Bill Masterson Memorial
GIVEN FOR: **perseverance, sportsmanship, and dedication**
NAMED FOR: **North Stars player who died after hitting head on ice in 1968**
2007–2008 WINNER: **Jason Blake, Toronto**
MOST WINS: **players only win once**

King Clancy Memorial
GIVEN FOR: **leadership and community contributions**
NAMED FOR: **Maple Leafs' player and coach**
2007–2008 WINNER: **Vincent Lecavalier, Tampa Bay**
MOST WINS: **players only win once**

Conn Smythe Trophy
GIVEN TO: **Stanley Cup playoffs most valuable player**
NAMED FOR: **Maple Leafs executive**
2007–2008 WINNER: **Henrik Zetterberg, Detroit**
MOST WINS: **several players with two**

Maurice Richard Trophy
GIVEN TO: **top goal scorer***
NAMED FOR: **Hall of Fame player known as "The Rocket"**
2007–2008 WINNER: **Alex Ovechkin, Washington**
MOST WINS: **2, Pavel Bure, Jarome Igilna**

*Established in 1999

BAD
Sports Records

Holding a sports record is usually a great honour. Being the best at something or having the most of something is normally something to brag about. However, there are some records in sports that no one wants to hold. But guess what? Someone has to! On these pages, read about some of the least popular records in sports and meet the unfortunate record-holders. You can look it up (but most of these folks would probably prefer you didn't!).

FOOTBALL

Most fumbles in a game
7, Len Dawson, 1964

Throwing most interceptions in a game
8, Jim Hardy, 1950

Throwing most interceptions in a season
42, George Blanda, 1962

Most times sacked in a season
76, David Carr, 2001

Most consecutive losses (team)
26, Tampa Bay Buccaneers, 1976–1977

BASEBALL

Most errors in an inning
6, Joe Mulvey (3B), 1884

Most errors in a career
972, Bill Dahlen (SS)

Most home runs allowed in a career
505, Robin Roberts

Most grounding into double plays, career
350, Cal Ripken, Jr.

Most strikeouts (by a batter) in a season
204, Mark Reynolds, 2008

Most losses in a season (team)
134, Cleveland Spiders, 1899

BASKETBALL

Worst free-throw percentage in a career (min. 1,200 free throws made)
Wilt Chamberlain, 51.1 percent

Most turnovers in a season
366, Artis Gilmore, 1977–1978

Most losses in a season (team)
73, Philadelphia 76ers, 1972–1973

HOCKEY

Most goals allowed by one team in game:
16, Quebec Bulldogs, vs. Montreal, March 3, 1920

Most penalty minutes in a season
472, Dave "Tiger" Schultz, 1974–1975

Most career losses by a goalie
352, Gump Worsley

HORSE RACING

Most consecutive losses
100, Zippy Chippy, 1992–2004

MAJOR LEAGUE
Soccer Champs

Inspired by the success of the 1994 soccer World Cup, held in the United States for the first time, Major League Soccer (MLS) was launched in 1996. It was not the first pro soccer league in America, but it has become the most successful. For the 2008 season, it had 14 teams playing across the country. Here is a list of winners of the annual MLS Cup, the league's championship.

YEAR	MLS CHAMPION
2008	Columbus Crew
2007	Houston Dynamo
2006	Houston Dynamo
2005	Los Angeles Galaxy
2004	D.C. United
2003	San Jose Earthquakes
2002	Los Angeles Galaxy
2001	San Jose Earthquakes
2000	Kansas City Wizards
1999	D.C. United
1998	Chicago Fire
1997	D.C. United
1996	D.C. United

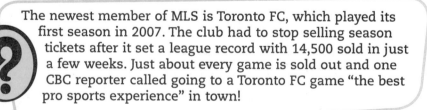

The newest member of MLS is Toronto FC, which played its first season in 2007. The club had to stop selling season tickets after it set a league record with 14,500 sold in just a few weeks. Just about every game is sold out and one CBC reporter called going to a Toronto FC game "the best pro sports experience" in town!

CANADIAN Soccer Clubs

The Canadian Soccer Association organizes hundreds of matches and tournaments for men, women, and youth players. Since 1984, they have kept detailed records of which clubs have been the most successful. They assigned points to each team's championship finishes and came up with the following chart, which includes tournaments through 2007. An "F" after a club means that they got all their points from girls' teams only.

TEAM, PROVINCE	POINTS
Lac St. Louis Lakers, QC	323
St. John's, NF	282
Dartmouth United, NS	253
Bonivital, MB	231
Scarborough United (F), ON	195
Rive Sud, QC	175
Burlington, ON	169
Lakeshore (F), QC	154
Burnaby, BC	153
Dynamo Quebec (F), QC	153
Oakville, ON	147

MR. AND MS.
Everythings

For some athletes, it's not enough to be world-class at just one sport. These multitalented superstars excelled in two or more sports. They didn't just play in other sports, they were among the best in both. The hardest part of their lives was probably keeping all the uniforms straight!

Jim Brown
Hall of Fame member in both NFL and college lacrosse

Bo Jackson
All-star baseball player; Pro Bowl running back

Eduoard (Newsy) Lalonde
Hockey Hall of Fame member; named top lacrosse player of first half of 20th century

Jackie Robinson
First four-sport star at UCLA; baseball Hall of Famer

Jim Thorpe
Olympic gold medal winner in heptathlon and decathlon; NFL Hall of Famer; pro baseball player

Hayley Wickenheiser
Olympic and pro hockey star; played softball for Canada at 2000 Olympics

Babe Didrikson Zaharias
Olympic champion in track; golfing superstar

Spoons & Niblicks!

Golfers today can carry 14 clubs in their golf bags during an official round. The three main types of clubs are woods (though they're all made of metal now), irons, and putters. The woods and irons are numbered, in most cases. You use a 1-wood, or driver, to tee off, then perhaps hit a 5-iron toward the green. Once on the green, you use a putter. In the early days of golf, however, all the clubs had names. They don't match up exactly with the numbered clubs of today in how they were made or what they looked like, but these are the approximate comparisons between yesterday (before the 1920s or so) and today. So, where did I put my niblick?

OLD NAME	SIMILAR CLUB TODAY
Play club	Driver
Brassie	2-wood
Spoon	3-4-5-woods
Baffing spoon	6-7-8-woods
Cleek	1- or 2-iron
Mid mashie	3-iron
Mashie iron	4-iron
Mashie	5-iron
Spade	6-iron
Mashie niblick	7-iron
Pitching niblick	8-iron
Niblick	9-iron
Jigger	Wedge
Putter (or blank)	Putter

Famous
Sports Streaks

The "streak" has always fascinated sports fans. An athlete's ability to succeed over and over again, against all the odds and opponents, places them above the rest. Some streaks are team achievements, when skill, determination, and yes, luck all come together to help a team win again and again. Here are some of the most famous streaks in sports history.

Baseball

Joe DiMaggio hit safely in 56 consecutive games, 1941.

Lou Gehrig played in 2,130 consecutive games, 1923–1939.

Cal Ripken, Jr., broke Gehrig's record with a total of 2,632, 1982–1998.

The Boston Red Sox won eight straight postseason games to win the World Series, 2004.

Basketball

The Los Angeles Lakers won 33 games in a row, 1971–1972.

UCLA's basketball team won 88 games in a row, 1971–1974, and nine of 10 NCAA basketball titles, 1964–1973.

Cycling

Lance Armstrong won seven straight Tour de France races, 1999–2005.

Football

The Miami Dolphins won 17 games in a row, the NFL's only undefeated season, 1972.

The University of Oklahoma won 47 straight games, 1953–1957.

Hockey

The Montreal Canadiens played in 11 straight Stanley Cup Finals, winning six, 1950–60.

Wayne Gretzky was the NHL's most valuable player eight straight years, 1980–1987.

Golf

Tiger Woods made the cut (qualified for the final rounds) in 142 consecutive tournaments, 1998–2005.

Tennis

Martina Navratilova set a women's record with 74 consecutive match victories, 1984.

Track and Field

Edwin Moses won 107 straight 400-metre hurdle races, 1977–1987.

So, which of these streaks is the most unbreakable? Fans of American sports would probably look to DiMaggio's record; since 1941, no player has come closer than 12 games to his mark. In team sports, UCLA's record is probably toughest, since few of the best players stay in college long enough to help break it. Around the world, Armstrong's mark is probably unbeatable. But you never know!

Tour de France
Champions

The Tour de France bicycle race is perhaps the most gruelling and difficult challenge in sports. Over the course of about a month, riders cover about 3,200 km (2,000 miles) in a series of daily rides, often climbing thousands of feet up steep mountain roads. The race demands great skill, enormous stamina, and supreme dedication. When American Lance Armstrong finally hung up his cycling helmet after winning his record seventh Tour in 2005, he found himself atop this list of multiple Tour de France winners.

Cyclist, Country	Tour de France Wins
Lance Armstrong, USA	7
Bernard Hinault, France	5
Eddy Merckx, Belgium	5
Miguel Indurain, Spain	5
Jacques Anquetil, France	5
Greg LeMond, USA	3
Louis Bobet, France	3
Phillipe Thys, Belgium	3

Figure Skating
MOVES

Every sport has its own language, of course, but figure skating seems to have some of the most colourful. Here is a list of some of the most well-known names of manoeuvres used by figure skaters during their routines.

TYPES OF JUMPS	TYPES OF SPINS
Axel	Biellman
Flip	Broken leg spin
Lutz	Camel
Salchow	Death drop spin
Toe loop	Flying camel
Walley	Flying sit spin
Waltz jump	Layback
	Sit spin

Your Name in Ice

Several of these moves take their name from their inventors. Ulrich Salchow won the world championship ten times early in the 20th century. Axel Paulson was the 1908 Olympic champion. Alois Lutz invented the jump that bears his name. American Dorothy Hamill perfected a version of an older trick; hers was dubbed a "Hamill Camel."

Odd Balls

Most sports use round (or should we say "spherical?") balls — golf balls, tennis balls, basketballs, bowling balls, volleyballs, etc. Footballs are a little different, of course. (Here's some great trivia for you, by the way. Do you know what the shape of a football is called? Amaze your friends by knowing that it's a "prolate spheroid.") But not every sport bounces to the tune of a round ball. Here's a list of some pieces of unusual sports equipment that are used sort of like a ball — they are thrown, kicked, batted, hit, or otherwise tossed — but look very little like the balls you're used to.

Birdie

Not thrown but hit with a badminton racket, birdies (or "shuttlecocks") are made of feathers or plastic and are shaped like cones.

Curling stone

Slid along the ice in the sport of curling, the round stone has a flat bottom and a handle on top.

Discus

Shaped like a bulging dinner plate, the discus is thrown after a spinning run-up.

Earthball

About 1.8 m (6 ft.) in diameter and made of canvas, it is used in playground games.

Hammer

A shot (see opposite page) at the end of a chain or wire; it is thrown after a spinning run-up.

Javelin

A thin, metal, spear-like pole thrown for distance.

Medicine ball

This is a heavy leather or plastic ball filled with sand or liquid that is used for exercising.

Road bowling ball

A solid iron ball about twice the size of a golf ball, this ball is used in an Irish sport that is contested on roads between towns.

Sepak takraw

Made of woven wicker, wood, or plastic, it is used in an Asian foot-tennis game.

Shot

An iron ball about the size of a five-pin bowling ball, it is thrown for distance in a track-and-field event.

Mega Moto X

Daring, brave, or just crazy — Moto X riders have taken the aerial stunts of BMX bicycles and turned them into high-flying, supercharged vertical ballets. Gunning their motorcycles off ramps, they fly through the air, doing any one of dozens of types of gymnastic tricks in midair. They land safely (we hope) and their moves are scored by judges. Here is how the hotshots do a few of the hot Moto X tricks you might see at events such as the X Games or Winter X Games.

Backflip
Do a 360-degree (complete circle) backward loop.

Bar Hop
Put both feet on the handlebars and then get them back down before landing.

Coffin
Lie on your back and hold your feet out forward, while still holding on to the handlebars.

Nothing
Take your hands and feet off the bike and then get them back on (quickly!) before landing.

Saran Wrap
Circle one foot under each hand, one after the other.

Superman
Keep your hands on the handlebars but straighten your body out parallel to the ground.

Twitch
Stick one leg out to the side and one leg over the handlebars while in flight.

Whip
Keep your hands and feet on the bike, but turn the bike so that it's "lying down" in midair; straighten up before landing.

Ironpeople

A triathlon is a race in which competitors swim, bike, and run over varying distances. The ultimate triathlon length is the mighty Ironman, the most famous of which is in Hawaii. In an Ironman triathlon, men and women first swim 3.8 km (2.4 miles) in an open, rough, and choppy ocean. Climbing out, they hop on racing bikes and pedal for 180 km (112 miles). They wrap up their day with a marathon — 42 km (26 miles, 385 yards) of gruelling running. The best can finish in about eight hours. That's a tough day at the office. Here's a list of the most successful Hawaii Ironman competitors since the first race in 1978.

IRONPERSON	NO. OF RACES WON
Paula Newby-Fraser	8
Dave Scott	6
Mark Allen	6
Natascha Badmann	6
Peter Reid	3
Tim DeBoom	2
Scott Tinley	2
Luc Van Lierde	2
Erin Baker	2
Lori Bowden	2
Chrissie Wellington	2

Sports Game Page

For our last game, we'll test your knowledge of the sports stuff you've read in this chapter. There are three "odd balls," five NASCAR families, three female athletes (last names only), four baseball teams, and five MLS teams. (For the teams, use nicknames; such as *Bears*, not *Chicago Bears*.) If you can't track them down without a list, check out the answer list on page 319 (but no peeking at the answer grid!).

```
R  S  N  A  I  D  N  I  Q  S  E  T
E  D  A  V  S  I  D  E  T  I  N  U
J  A  V  E  L  I  N  I  E  O  L  W
O  L  R  S  T  P  G  W  A  T  L  A
N  L  A  R  Q  E  T  N  O  B  A  L
E  I  T  D  R  T  E  F  N  I  B  L
S  M  I  S  A  T  D  Z  V  F  H  A
G  A  L  A  X  Y  A  W  W  L  T  C
S  H  O  R  A  H  A  Z  I  O  R  E
H  A  V  M  A  L  X  O  Z  C  A  Y
R  E  A  R  T  H  Q  U  A  K  E  S
E  F  I  R  D  E  I  N  R  D  X  T
D  A  I  L  R  J  G  I  D  M  Y  H
S  P  M  I  S  E  D  I  S  C  U  S
O  O  F  D  L  E  D  V  T  A  S  U
X  O  S  S  E  J  L  S  H  E  N  E
```

Index

Games Answer Page

HISTORY, page 44

1. 1918
2. 1986
3. 360
4. 1979
5. 1497
6. 1932
7. 1917
8. 1970
9. 1988
10. 1944

```
1 1 9 8 7 4 0 7 1 1 3 4
2 3 9 1 3 2 8 5 9 1 0 1
8 1 4 9 7 0 4 2 1 7 1 9
9 8 7 4 5 1 2 3 7 9 8 1
1 8 9 4 0 9 6 6 0 1 9 8
1 9 4 4 7 9 2 0 1 4 3 0
9 1 4 5 8 0 9 6 1 9 3 2
7 4 0 3 5 8 1 9 7 9 2 9
0 6 8 9 1 8 3 6 5 0 1 0
```

SOCIAL STUDIES, page 76

1. Human Resources
2. Comoros
3. Sable Island
4. Sri Lanka
5. Ontario
6. Subway
7. Andorra
8. Malta
9. Public Safety
10. Cromwell

Phrase: Social Studies rocks!

WORLD AND WEATHER, page 104

Here are the "out of place" words and the list topics:

1. Stremco, Emissions
2. Barriers, Mountains
3. Malta, Smallest Countries by Pop.
4. Sealand, Are We There Yet?
5. Buttertown, Places with Food Names
6. Miami, Active Volcanoes
7. Al-Aqsa, Driest Places
8. Gordon, People Who Went Around the World (last names)
9. Monkey, Types of Maps
10. Corks, Names of Seashells

SCIENCE, page 136

Here are the ten "triple matches."

Andromeda, Astronomy, Galaxy,
Element, Chemistry, Gas
Deca, Math, Power
Stratum corneum, Dermatology,
Dermis
Incisors, Dentistry, Canine
Ethanol, Power, Corn
Cloning, DNA, Sheep
Dinosaur, Paleontology,
Antarctosaurus
CAT, Tomography, Doctor
Eucalyptus, Botanic, Specimen

WORDS, page 168

POP CULTURE, page 196

Beatles
Austin Powers
Robin Williams
Tiki Barber
Severus Snape
Ice Cube
Maxwell Smart
Pink
Stephen King
Oprah Winfrey
Nancy Drew

Answer: Bart Simpson

ANIMALS, page 224

1. deer
2. rhino
3. ostrich
4. hermit crab
5. bison
6. narwhal
7. lab rat
8. tetra
9. arachnid

Secret animal: human beings

FOOD, page 248

The mixed up meal is,
Chicken
Asparagus
Mashed Potatoes
Milk
Cheesecake

GRAB BAG, page 276

1. vomitologist
2. Wat Pho Buddha
3. Conor
4. A. Janus; B. Sunne;
   C. Emperor; D. Roman

Mystery word: humectant

SPORTS, page 308

Answers:

Galaxy	Waltrip
United	Labonte
Earthquakes	Flock
Wizards	Zaharias
Fire	Hamill
Javelin	Navratilova
Earthball	Indians
Discus	Red Sox
Wallace	Tigers
Petty	Angels

Signing Off

At the end of TV programs — mostly news shows, but some fictional shows — the hosts or newscasters often use well-known phrases to say goodbye or good night. Some have created catchphrases that have stood the test of time (mostly!). Here are some famous "sign-offs" from TV history (plus one movie). And now . . . it's our turn to sign-off. We'll just use, "See ya later, alligator!"

"And that's the way it is."
—Walter Cronkite, CBS News

"Good night and good news."
—Ted Baxter (Ted Knight) on *The Mary Tyler Moore Show*

"For now, Dick Clark — so long."
—Dick Clark on *American Bandstand*

"See you on the radio."
—Charles Osgood, *CBS This Morning*

"Good night and good luck."
—Edward R. Murrow on radio and TV

"And so it goes."
—Linda Ellerbee on *NickNews*

"Seacrest . . . out!"
—Ryan Seacrest on *American Idol*
(though it didn't last long as a sign-off!)

"Stay classy, San Diego."
—Ron Burgundy (Will Ferrell) in *Anchorman*

 The comic team of George Burns and Gracie Allen had a great sign-off. Allen's character was, well, not too bright. At the end of their shows, Burns would say, "Say good night, Gracie." And she'd say, "Good night, Gracie!" Get it? Later!